For the Love of Our Husbands

52 Devotions for Wives and Prayers for the Men They Love

Darby Dugger

CROSSBOOKS
PUBLISHING

CrossBooks™
A Division of LifeWay
1663 Liberty Drive
Bloomington, IN 47403
www.crossbooks.com
Phone: 1-866-879-0502

First published by CrossBooks 6/21/2011

ISBN: 978-1-6150-7863-9 (sc)
ISBN: 978-1-6150-7864-6 (dj)

Library of Congress Control Number: 2011928982

Printed in the United States of America

This book is printed on acid-free paper.

Certain stock imagery © Thinkstock.
Any people depicted in stock imagery provided by Thinkstock are models, and such images are being used for illustrative purposes only.

Cover photo provided by Tyler Michael Pelan.

Acknowledgments

There are so many people who have supported me throughout this endeavor. Without their encouragement, this book would not be. So, from the bottom of my heart I would like to thank:

My amazing husband, Jason Alan Dugger. I am honored to be your wife and am spurred toward excellence because of your example. Thank you for believing in me and helping me achieve my dream. I love you!

Erin Clark, who not only named the book, but without whose prompting there would be no book. I love you, sister!

Laurie Allen, Julie Dabney, Christie Heller, Karissa Sites, and Beth Stone. You have been wonderful friends, examples, and mentors to me in my quest to be a godly wife. Thank you for living out the Proverbs 31 woman!

All the women who came alongside of me in 2009 to pray daily for our husbands. Without your accountability and advice I would not have been as persistent in my prayers. Thank you for journeying with me.

Introduction

I've never been one to make New Year's resolutions, mainly because I am never able to keep up with them. Essentially, a New Year's resolution is an attempt to better myself, *by* myself. When I am tempted to skip a workout, sleep late instead of reading my Bible, or forgo whatever resolution I have made, there is no one to hold me accountable. After years of unsuccessful resolutions, I had simply given up on making even a feeble attempt at improvement, knowing that it would never stick.

My husband, Jason, and I had been married almost four years when we were blessed with our first child, Havana, in October of 2008. Though we had not been married very long, I loved my role as a wife. I enjoyed praying for Jason and serving him in every way. However, it wasn't long after the birth of our daughter that I realized the majority of my thoughts, actions, and prayers were now directed toward her. Of course, I still loved Jason very much, but I am embarrassed to admit that he took a backseat in our family. So when New Year's rolled around a few months later, a friend suggested I pray very specifically each day for my husband. I made it my resolution.

Knowing that I couldn't achieve my goal alone, I e-mailed a small group of friends to ask if they would join me in this resolution and help hold me accountable. I decided to send out a weekly e-mail that included a challenge to help me improve as a wife and a prayer for Jason I intended to pray every day that week. I had no idea how quickly these e-mails would spread. This small group of friends quickly multiplied and before I knew it, nearly one hundred women were receiving my weekly e-mails. My simple New Year's resolution had turned into a ministry that not only changed me and my marriage, but impacted many other marriages as well. That is why I've created this book, in the hope that you will see God work in your marriage through this same collection of e-mails. I am so thankful that you are joining me on this journey.

In the following pages, you will find the weekly e-mails I composed. Each devotion is divided up into two sections. A "challenge" section which is aimed at us in our roles as wives. The point of this section is to highlight areas in which we as wives might be able to improve and become more like the Biblical model of wifehood. Some of the themes will be aimed towards marriage and others will focus on our walks with Christ. While the challenges are specific to my marriage, I hope that you will take them and make them your own. My hope is that, through my suggestions, you are able to apply them to your marriage in a way that is meaningful to you.

Following the challenge is a section entitled "For the Love of My Husband." In this section you will find a specific Scripture-based prayer that you should try to pray for your husband every day of the week. Again, these prayers are meant to be personalized and expanded upon based on your particular situation. This will help develop a habit of praying Scripture daily for your husband and fighting for him upon your knees. Some weeks the theme for the challenge and the prayer will coordinate; many weeks they won't. I wanted to make sure that our husbands were thoroughly covered in prayers specific to their needs as a men, husbands, and fathers and often times those were not the same things that challenge us as wives.

Again, thank you for joining me on this journey! Praying the Truth for our husbands is very powerful, and I am certain that God wants to accomplish great things in our marriages. I will be praying for you, and I ask that you pray for me. Let's do this together—for the love of our husbands!

Challenge

Do you struggle to pray regularly and specifically for your husband? I do. I wish I could say that I purposefully pray for his relationship with the Lord, his role as a husband and father, his career, his future, or any other needs (present or future) that he might have in his life. But oftentimes, several days will pass before I remember to say even a sentence of prayer specifically for him. I wish this wasn't the case, and, with the Lord's help, I am determined to change my patterns and my prayer life, so that I can truly be a woman of prayer for the love (and sake!) of my husband. I can't imagine a better way to show my love for him than to invite the Creator of the Universe into the depths of his life.

I love music. I constantly keep my stereo or iPod playing to provide a soundtrack for my day. Even riding in the car without playing the radio is difficult for me! So my challenge this week is to examine my life and see what distractions can be sacrificed in order to make room for a more prayerful lifestyle. Music is clearly the choice for me, but perhaps for you it is your TV, computer, or phone. These don't have to be completely eliminated from our daily routine, but this week, instead of doing the dishes to music, I will be doing the dishes to prayer!

Precious Father, I pray that You would help me as I seek to eliminate the distractions in my life that take time away from talking with You. Lord, grant me the discipline to turn my thought life into prayer time for the man I love. Help me quiet my life in order to listen and talk with You. I pray these things in Your Son's name. Amen.

For the Love of My Husband

Dear Lord, I pray that you would come and meet my husband where he is today. I pray that he would confidently proclaim, like Peter, that Jesus is the Christ, the Son of the Living God (Matthew 16:16). May he choose the way of truth and set his heart on Your laws (Psalm 119:3). I pray that this year he will grow by leaps and bounds in his faith and that he will experience Your presence in his life more intimately than ever before. It is in Jesus' name, I pray. Amen.

Week 2

Challenge

Sometimes I find that my house breeds chaos and tension. You see, I am usually running behind on my lengthy "to do" list, and the task of keeping up can be quite stressful. When Jason comes home from work, I often bark orders at him or whine about my day without giving him a chance to unwind physically or emotionally. Currently, Jason is in his third year of medical residency. His work hours can be brutal, and despite the fact that I know he is exhausted, I often fail to create a restful atmosphere for him at home.

My challenge for this week stems from a line in Stormie Omartian's book, *The Power of a Praying Wife*. In this book, she prays, "Help me to create a peaceful, restful, safe place for him to come home to."[1] I desire our home to be just that. With God's help, I will not nag or speak negatively toward my husband; I will use my words to build him up. I will greet him with a smile and provide time for him to unwind before I give him a list of things that need to be done or ask him to watch our daughter—no matter how tired I am. I will make our home a safe retreat for him after the difficulties of his day. Our husbands need to feel welcomed and appreciated in their own homes, and I will foster that type of environment for Jason.

Sweet Jesus, thank You for showing me areas where I can improve as a wife. Please help me as I strive to create a restful environment in our home for my husband. Help my attitudes and actions build my husband up and help me learn to put him and his needs before my own desires. Thank You, and it is in Your name that I pray. Amen.

For the Love of My Husband

Father God, I pray, according to Your Word, that You would give my husband the strength to lead. Help him as he leads us spiritually, financially, and in every area of our marriage and parenting. I pray that he would be strong and courageous. Help him obey Your Word and not turn away from it to the right or to the left, that he may be successful wherever he goes (Joshua 1:7). May Your commands be upon his heart so that he can impress them upon our family. Help him lead us in honorable discussions when we sit at home and drive along the road, when we get up and go to sleep (Deuteronomy 6:6–7). Thank You for placing him at the head of our home, and please grant me a submissive heart to show him respect with my attitude, actions, and words. Thank You for my husband! In Jesus' name, I pray. Amen.

Week 3

Challenge

Yesterday, I was convicted of having too many expectations of my husband. As I reflected on this topic, I realized that whenever I become upset with Jason, it is usually because an expectation of mine has not been met. I may want him to do or say something specific but I don't necessarily express my wishes to him verbally. Then, when he doesn't deliver on my expectations, my feelings are hurt. Is that fair to him? No. Is he a mind-reader? No. Are some of my expectations unrealistic? *Yes!*

A recent example of this in my life may sound silly, but the principle applies to most arguments in our home. The other day, Jason met a friend for lunch at a local Indian restaurant. Now, Jason knows that I love Indian food, and I assumed that he would order a "to-go" lunch and bring it home for me to enjoy. Yet, when Jason came home, he didn't have any food with him. My feelings were deeply hurt when he returned with nothing more than the smell of curry on his breath! My husband was caught off guard by my disappointment because I never *asked* him to order a lunch for me. "How was I supposed to know?" he argued. In my heart, I knew that he was right, but I still found myself irritated with him. Perhaps it was my hunger, but more than likely it was my unmet expectation. Therefore, my challenge this week is to keep my expectations in check. When there is something I want or need, I will clearly communicate it to my husband instead of assuming that he already knows. I will pray that I show my husband respect and love through my actions and that I develop realistic expectations of him in our marriage.

Dear Lord, help me to develop realistic expectations for my marriage. I am sorry for the times when I bring tension into the home through my unrealistic or uncommunicated desires. May I openly and clearly communicate with my husband about my needs and concerns, and allow me to have grace when some of them can't be fulfilled. I pray all of these things in Your name. Amen.

For the Love of My Husband

Father God, thank You for my husband. I pray that he will hunger and thirst for righteousness (Matthew 5:6), that he will love You with all of his heart, mind, soul, and strength (Mark 12:30), and that he would hate what is evil and cling to what is good (Romans 12:9). Help him to be still and know that You are God, and use him to exalt Your name among the nations (Psalm 46:10). Give him the discipline to spend the quality time with You each day where he can experience Your goodness and kindness. Draw him near to You, Lord. I pray that he would choose to honor You with his life and put You above me and our children. I pray that my husband's love for You would be reflected in his relationship with others and that many may come to know You as they experience Your love through him. In Your Son's name, I pray. Amen.

Week 4

Challenge

Sometimes it feels like anything that *can* go wrong *will* go wrong. That principle accurately describes our lives this week in the Dugger home. Lately it seems that Jason and I have experienced many stressors pulling us in different directions. Jason's work has kept him extremely busy for the past two weeks, and I am often tired of feeling like a single mom because of the long hours he works. On top of that, we recently had a friend lose his battle with cancer, and our daughter was diagnosed with early-onset stranger anxiety, which can be embarrassing and stressful whenever we are in public. Unfortunately, the sum of these circumstances has left us both irritable and short-tempered.

My challenge this week is to see things from my husband's point of view and to pray for myself to be "quick to listen, slow to speak, and slow to become angry" (James 1:19). Sometimes I find myself taking out my frustrations on Jason when he is not really the source. With God's help, I can bite my tongue and see things from Jason's perspective. Instead of focusing on how challenging it is to be a stay-at-home mother, I can remember that my husband is a man who works hard to support his family, who is physically exhausted from his job, and who is often sad that he can't spend more time with us. Setting aside time daily to pray for him will enable me to partner with my husband during our most stressful moments instead of using him as an emotional punching bag.

Holy Father, We live in a world that is slow to listen, quick to speak, and quick to become angry. I pray that you would grant me strength to do the opposite. May I be quick to listen, slow to speak, and slow to become angry. Allow that wise verse to penetrate my heart and influence my actions. Help me to see more of my husband's viewpoint on a situation and forgive me for the times when I am selfish and only look at things from my side. I ask this in the name of Your Son. Amen.

For the Love of My Husband

Father God, in the name of Jesus Christ, I come before You today and ask for Your hand of protection over my husband. I pray that You would bind Satan from him and cover my husband in the precious blood of Jesus. Lord, please protect his mind, heart, and soul from Satan's lies and schemes. I pray that my husband would be self-controlled and alert so that the Devil cannot devour him (1 Peter 5:8). May my husband put on full armor daily—the belt of truth, the breastplate of righteousness, the sandals that are the gospel of peace, the helmet of salvation, the sword of the Spirit, and especially the shield of faith—so that he can extinguish the flaming arrows of the Evil One (Ephesians 6:10–17). Lord, we know that temptations will come, but please allow my husband to see the way out that You have provided (1 Corinthians 10:13), and grant him the strength and desire to choose that path. I pray that, like You, he would fight Satan's attacks with Your Word, which is perfect and everlasting. Thank You for the example You provided when You came to earth. Please help my husband stand firm against the Evil One. Protect our family, starting with him, and fill him with Your Spirit, from the top of his head to the soles of his feet. I ask all of these things in the mighty and holy name of Christ. Amen.

Week 5

Challenge

Although I can already see a difference in myself and my marriage since I began praying for Jason every day, I realize there are many times that I allow negative thoughts to invade my mind-set. Personally, it is very easy for me to dwell on past disappointments in my marriage instead of taking every thought captive as we are instructed in 2 Corinthians 10:5. Whenever I hold on to those negative moments or relive them in my mind, Satan quickly takes advantage and begins whispering lies into my spirit. Few things can tear down our mate faster than rehashing his past mistakes, and God has called us to forgive our husbands just as we have been forgiven. Furthermore, we are taught in Ephesians 4:27 not to do anything that would give Satan a foothold, but when I dwell on negative thoughts and memories, I am providing Satan an opportunity to plant his seed of destruction in my marriage. My challenge this week is to become more intentional about taking every thought captive. If my thoughts aren't from Christ, then I must dismiss them quickly from my mind. I want to have a more optimistic and God-honoring attitude in my marriage.

Father God, please help me as I take every thought captive. Help me have the wisdom to understand if the thought is constructive or destructive for my marriage. If it is destructive, enable me to dismiss it from my mind immediately. I pray that you would help me focus on the positive and not dwell on past hurts. May I never give Satan a foothold in my thought life and in my marriage. I pray all of these things in Jesus' name. Amen.

For the Love of My Husband

Sweet Jesus, thank You for my family and especially for my husband. I pray that during times of transition, he would remember that You are the same yesterday, today, and forever (Hebrews 13:8) and that you do not change like shifting shadows (James 1:17). Pour out Your Spirit on him and grant him a vision (Joel 2:28) for our family that is pleasing to You. Lord, I pray that You not only grant my husband this vision, but that You also give him a passion to accomplish the tasks You have laid before him. Help him maintain an eternal mindset and continually make the best decisions for our family and for Your kingdom purposes. Guide him in the way of wisdom and lead him along straight paths (Proverbs 4:11). May his vision have nothing to do with selfish ambition or vain conceit, but may he model Your humility and selfless love (Philippians 2:3, 5). Use my husband to minister to those who are lost and hurting, and may that be the goal of our entire family, more than financial security, happiness, or success. I love You, Lord, and I thank You for Your grace. I pray all of these things in Your name. Amen.

Week 6

Challenge

Are you ever driven by your emotions? I am. I often allow my feelings to influence my behaviors; however, this isn't ideal. A mentor once told me, "Feelings follow actions." By this, she meant that if we do loving things for our husbands even when we don't feel like it, the emotions of love will soon follow. She encouraged me not to base my actions toward Jason solely on how I feel, but rather show him love and respect and allow the feelings to follow.

I don't know about you, but for me, this can be a difficult task. Last week I was ashamed at how often my mind dwelt on negative thoughts. To honor the previous challenge, I tried to take every thought captive, and I tried not to think or speak destructive things toward Jason. I realized that I rarely noticed what Jason had done right; instead, I often focused on what he *failed* to do. This was a sobering thought. In an effort to change my mindset, I sent Jason an e-mail with the subject "What You Did Right," and I listed specific things he had done that I appreciated. I don't know what prompted me to write this list, other than the fact that I was frustrated with my inability to take every thought captive and truly dismiss the thoughts that weren't beneficial to our marriage. I certainly love Jason with all my heart and think he is an incredible husband, but why is it so hard for me to express that to him?

Jason greatly appreciated the e-mail I sent, and I noticed that my feelings did, in fact, follow my actions. Writing that list changed my perspective and allowed me to focus on things about Jason that I had previously chosen to ignore. With these attributes in mind, I certainly began to feel more loved and appreciated by Jason, and, consequently, it deepened my love and respect for him. This week, my challenge is to remember that feelings follow actions and to show my husband how much I appreciate him despite my emotions.

Precious Father, thank You for the people who speak truth into my life. I pray that "feelings follow actions" will be a motto I can live by and apply daily to my marriage. Strengthen my resolve to take notice of all that my husband does instead of what he might not be doing. May my actions towards Jason never be based on my feelings or circumstances, and allow me to choose to act lovingly and give to him even when I don't feel like it. Thank You, Jesus, for choosing to take my punishment for sin even though You wanted the cup to pass from you. It is in Your name that I pray. Amen.

For the Love of My Husband

Father God, You are referred to as the God of Peace throughout the Bible, and I pray that You would be exactly that for my husband right now. When You walked this earth, You calmed a storm with merely the sound of Your voice (Matthew 8:23–27). I pray that with that same voice, You would calm every storm within my husband's heart and mind today. You tell us that we will find rest for our souls in You alone because Your yoke is easy and Your burden is light (Matthew 11:29–30). Thank You for that amazing promise! I pray that my husband would comprehend that truth and relinquish his burdens to You. Thank You for giving us an eternal peace that does not pass away, no matter how difficult our circumstances may be. I pray that my husband would not be afraid or troubled, but that he would take heart, being confident that You have overcome the world and that You, Yourself, are peace (John 14:27, John 16:33, Ephesians 2:14). May the peace that transcends all comprehension (Philippians 4:7) abundantly fill my husband. I pray that he would know Your character just as Gideon did when he built an altar and named it "The Lord is Peace" (Judges 6:24). Thank You for truly being the God of Peace. I love You, Lord, and I ask all of these things in Jesus' name. Amen.

Week 7

Challenge

How much quality time do you spend with your spouse? Notice that the question wasn't how much *time* you spend with him, but how much *quality* time—whether you are making the most out of every moment that you share together.

My challenge this week is to remember that it isn't the *quantity* of time together that it is important, but the *quality*. Whether it is work, travel, children, ministries, or simply life in general, we all have obstacles that prevent us from spending as much time with our spouse as we would like. I want to make the most of the time that I share with my husband so that a small amount of quality time may be as fulfilling as a large quantity of time. Of course, that will require me to continue taking every thought captive, to not speak negatively, and to do the little things around the house that my husband appreciates. Dying to myself, serving my husband, and putting his needs, desires, and preferences before mine will create an atmosphere conducive to quality time together, even if it is brief or only over the phone.

Lord, grant me the wisdom to know how to spend wisely the limited time I get with my husband. I ask that You would magnify our time together so that a little time will feel like a lot of time. Draw us closer to each other in those brief moments, and give us a longing for each other when we are apart. I pray that you would meet both of our needs completely. I love you, Lord, and I pray these things in Jesus' Name. Amen.

For the Love of My Husband

Father, thank You for being omnipresent (Jeremiah 23:24, Psalm 139:8). I pray that during the times when my husband and I are apart we would remember that You are present with both of us. Use this time to draw us closer to You and help us remember that You are the only one who meets all of our needs. Please strengthen us as a couple and help us to appreciate each other even more. I pray that You would bless my husband and help him feel secure in my love for him despite our distance. No matter where my husband is right now, I pray, Lord, that You would whisper Your truths into his heart. I pray that he can sense Your Spirit and that he is kept safe in You. Please allow no harm to come to him and no disaster to come upon this house (Psalm 91:10). Protect him with Your Mighty Hand. Keep him from temptation and help me to be a wife deserving of my husband's full confidence and trust (Proverbs 31:11). Please help us use these times apart for edification as we draw closer to you. In Jesus' name, I pray. Amen.

Week 8

Challenge

How would you define *surrender*? I love the way Eric and Leslie Ludy describe surrender in their book, *The First 90 Days of Marriage*. They state, "Surrender is not a onetime act; it is a daily, moment-by-moment decision."[2] In other words, to surrender my life to God, I must continuously relinquish any hopes, dreams, or ambitions that are not in harmony with His will and daily submit my life under His authority. Through the act of surrendering, I can become more mature in my faith and understanding of God's plan for my life.

I have often prayed that God would help me become a better wife. Throughout my marriage, He has consistently answered those prayers by impressing upon my heart that, in order to mature as a wife, I must first mature as a Christian woman. Through the process of spiritual growth, He changes my heart in a manner that impacts all of my relationships. I believe this is God's blueprint for genuine change in my role as a wife. My challenge, then, is to live each moment completely surrendered to Christ. Indeed, it is not a onetime act. I will have to continually put to death my human nature in order to remain in that place of surrender, but I know the rewards will far outweigh any sacrifices.

Lord, I confess that I don't surrender my life under Your will as often as I should. Help me to change that. May I fully understand that surrendering to You is not a one-time act, but a decision I must make each moment of the day. Convict me when I am not following through this with challenge, as I know that by becoming a more faithful woman it will help me to become a better wife. I love You, Lord, and I surrender my life under Your authority. It is in Jesus' name I pray. Amen.

For the Love of My Husband

Father God, I pray that my husband would be sensitive to Your Spirit. I pray that, he would continually live out his faith in You. Help him put to death his sinful nature (Colossians 3:5) so that his life will echo Yours. Implant Your heart, Your mind, Your vision, Your love, Your joy, Your peace, Your

14

strength, and Your passion into his very being. Thank You, Lord, for pursuing my husband and making him more like You. I am confident that You will complete the good work that You have begun in his life (Philippians 1:6). In Jesus' precious name, I pray! Amen.[3]

Week 9

Challenge

This week's challenge might sound simple to some, but it is one that the Lord has recently laid on my heart. I want to get back in the habit of looking nice for Jason daily, not only when we go out in public. No, I'm not talking about the idealized 1950s housewife who touches up her makeup and ties a ribbon in her hair just before her husband comes home from work (I know that some of you were thinking that). I am simply talking about making an effort to look nice even when I'm staying home all day. While I certainly don't feel like I've "let myself go," I do put less effort into looking nice on days when we don't leave the house. In fact, I have become particularly good at wearing pajamas all day with the excuse that I have a four-month-old who is constantly peeing, pooping, or puking on me. I certainly think there is something positive about the comfort of marriage and the ability to be around your spouse without obsessing over your appearance, but as I was studying the Proverbs 31 woman, I came to the conclusion that she simply would not wear her pajamas all day. Even if my husband *does* find me attractive in a sweatshirt covered with spit-up, that doesn't mean I can't show him love by taking care of my appearance. It might not be convenient (more loads of laundry, having my hair pulled by a little girl while wearing it down instead of in a ponytail, etc.), but it is a gift I can give Jason to show him honor and respect. If he thinks baggy t-shirts and sweat pants are sexy, he's in for a real treat! During the extra time it will take to prepare myself in the mornings, I will be praying for my husband to know the Lord as his Creator.

Precious Father, thank You for creating me and making me perfect in Your sight. I pray that I will be more faithful in taking time to look nice for my husband. I pray that I would never become lazy in my desire to please my husband in every way, including my appearance. Help me as I find new ways to look nice, and remind me to put in the extra effort even when I'm not leaving the house. I pray that, through my efforts, my husband would delight in me as his wife. In Your Son's name, I pray. Amen.

For the Love of My Husband

Father God, I praise You for my husband, and I thank You for creating him in Your image (Genesis 1:26). I pray that he would truly understand that he is fearfully and wonderfully made (Psalm 139:14). Help him recognize that You have designed him inside and out. You have blessed him with many talents. May he use those gifts solely for Your glory. Thank You, Lord, for creating him with a very specific purpose. I pray that my husband can sense Your higher calling on his life and that he will fulfill every good purpose which You have planned out in advance for him to do (Ephesians 2:10). I ask that You reveal Yourself more to him each day through Your Creation, the people he interacts with (especially me) and the sights that he sees. May he catch glimpses of Your glory and worship You as his loving Creator! I love You, Father, and ask these things in the holy name of Jesus! Amen.

Week 10

Challenge

Is sin blocking the effectiveness of your prayers? My challenge for this week stems from a Stormie Omartian quote: "God sees things we don't. He knows where we have room for improvement. He doesn't have to search long to uncover attitudes and habits that are outside His perfect will for us. He requires us to not sin in our hearts because sin separates us from Him and we don't get our prayers answered."[4] Recently, God has brought to my mind specific times I have sinned yet have not repented. Jesus set a high standard for us when He redefined sin in the New Testament. According to His teaching, even lust is equal with adultery and hate is as sinful as murder (Matthew 5:21–30)! Wow. My challenge, then, is to ask God to show me any sin in my life that may be hindering my prayers. Repenting of our sins may not seem like a very "fun" challenge, but it is one that will make our prayers for our husbands far more effective.

Sweet Jesus, please forgive me for the times when I am callused to my own sin. I pray for Your Spirit to whisper into the hardest and darkest places of my heart. Help me bring to You any unrepented sin. Thank You for the complete forgiveness You offer, and help me as I seek to make my relationship right with You before praying for my husband. I pray that I would be sensitive to Your leading and Your correcting. May my life echo Yours. I pray these things in Your name. Amen.

For the Love of My Husband

Lord, I lift my husband up to You and pray that, according to Your Word, You would bless his work (Psalm 90:17) and show him how to honor You daily in his attitude and spirit. I pray that You would be Lord over my husband's career; may it be ordained, secure, and successful. May he not be lacking in diligence, but serve You with passion and enthusiasm (Romans 12:11). Grant him confidence in the gifts You've entrusted to him so that he may seek, find, and do good work. I pray he is exactly where You want him. If he is not, please tug at his heart and lead him in the right direction. While I hope that he finds his career fulfilling, I pray that he finds true satisfaction in serving You.

Whatever he does, may he work at it with all his heart, as working for You and not for man (Colossians 3:23). In Jesus' name, I pray. Amen.

Week 11

Challenge

Let's be honest; isn't it hard to submit to our husbands? Before I was married, I imagined it would be a *joy* to submit to my spouse. Now that I am married, however, I admit that it is easier said than done. While there are times that submitting brings me joy, more often than not, I find it difficult. I'll bet I am not the only one who struggles with genuine submission to my husband. One of my favorite quotes regarding submission is from Kimberly Hahn's book, *Chosen and Cherished.* She writes:

> Wifely submission is active obedience; it is not passivity. A wife's submission is rooted in her love and submission to the Lord first and to her husband second. ... A wife's submission to her husband strengthens his ability to lead. She cannot wait until she thinks he is worthy of such respect or trust before she follows him. She responds to his leadership in ordinary concerns and spiritual matters. Her response calls forth his responsibility before God. [5]

I love how Hahn defines submission here. She illustrates both the action and the purpose of submission, emphasizing that it strengthens our husband's ability to lead. How can my husband lead if I'm not allowing him to do so? Therefore, my challenge this week is to be more diligent in my active role of submitting and to obediently rise to this calling that God has given me as a wife.

Father God, submission is hard, but I know that with You all things are possible. I pray that You would help me as I seek to be submissive to my husband. Remind me that, by doing so, I will help him be the leader You have called him to be. Help me never underestimate my role as a submissive wife. As I submit my life to You, allow me also to submit to my husband. Thank You, Jesus, and it is in Your name that I pray. Amen.

For the Love of My Husband

Heavenly Father, thank You so much for the treasure that my husband is. I pray that, like Solomon, You would give him wisdom, insight, and a breadth of understanding as measureless as the sand on the seashore (1 Kings 4:29). I pray that he will not limit wisdom to himself (Job 15:8), but that he would seek You and Your Word, being confident that You give wisdom generously to those who ask (James 1:5). May he know that fearing You is the beginning of all wisdom (Psalm 111:10) and that from Your mouth comes knowledge and understanding (Proverbs 2:6). As my husband makes decisions every day, big and small, I pray that You would grant him wisdom and that he would seek Your counsel. I ask for all of these things in Your Son's name. Amen.

Week 12

Challenge

Our family makes a priority of investing time in the lives of others. Whether we are volunteering in our church or participating in short term mission trips, we enjoy each opportunity to share God's love with those in need. I wonder, though, how my family is affected if I spend all of my time and energy investing in others but neglect to invest in my husband?

A few months ago, I planned a romantic evening for Jason. However, "life" seemed to thwart my plans. That night, Jason came home from work feeling ill, so I decided to postpone my idea. The next evening, I stayed late at church for a meeting and came home exhausted. The third night was spent hosting a couple at our home who had joined our church recently. Do you see the pattern? Every night seemed to produce another obstacle, and I routinely found an excuse not to make the effort to romance Jason. Now, two months later, I *still* haven't put my idea into action! That proves to me that I am not investing in my husband and making him a priority as I should. My challenge this week is to make Jason my priority; I need to invest my time and energy in him before my other obligations. While I don't have to decline everything or everyone else that demands my attention, I might have to say no to some things—even if they are worthy of my time—in order to say yes to my husband.

Father God, I pray that You would be first in my life, but that my husband would be next, before my children or friends. Help me learn to budget my time and activities in order to allow my husband to be the person I invest in the most. I pray that You will convict me when my priorities are misplaced. Help me find contentment and joy in being the wife You want me to be. It is in Your name that I pray. Amen.

For the Love of My Husband

Father God, I ask You to be my husband's strength and his shield; may he trust in You and receive Your help. May his heart leap for joy and give thanks to You in song, for You, O Lord, are his strength and his fortress of salvation. Be his shepherd and carry him forever (Psalm 28:7–9). In Jesus' name, I pray. Amen!

Week 13

Challenge

When Jason and I were engaged, we made it clear to each other that divorce would *never* be an option. There is not an "out" available in our marriage. We have agreed that our vows are for life, no matter what challenges may arise. That is such a wonderful and freeing promise which has already helped us through some difficult times. While Jason and I agree wholeheartedly on this issue, he is much better about verbalizing it than I am. He has always been good at communicating to me, both verbally and in writing, that he will never leave me. I tell Jason that I love him every day, but I don't tell him nearly as often that I'll never leave him. Instead, I simply assume that he knows how committed I am because I tell him that I love him. However, love is an emotion and commitment is a decision. If it is important to him to continually express his commitment, then I need to do a better job at communicating it in return. My challenge this week is to become better at verbalizing not only my love, but also my *commitment* to my husband and our marriage.

Father God, help me as I seek to communicate my commitment to my husband. Allow me never to waiver in that commitment or neglect to express it. I pray that You would continue to impress upon my heart the importance of the marriage commitment so that I might never stray from expressing it or believing in it. Thank You for the sanctity of the marriage institution. I love You, Lord, and pray these things in Your Son's name. Amen.

For the Love of My Husband

Sweet Jesus, thank You for taking my place on the cross! I am humbled that You came to this earth, lived a sinless life (despite being tempted), and chose to endure emotional and physical pain as You were betrayed, beaten, and killed. All this so that we might join You in heaven one day! Your love for us is more than amazing. I pray this week that You would show more of Your deep and abiding love to my husband. May he look at the cross and the empty tomb with fresh eyes. May the story never grow old or become too familiar to him. I pray that it brings him to tears and to his knees each time he thinks of Your sacrifice.

May he rest in Your love and be secure in Your forgiveness knowing that it is a free gift. Thank You, Lord, for the work You completed on the cross! I pray that my husband would be more amazed at Your loving sacrifice than he has ever been before. Continue to show him Your unconditional love, and allow him to experience a fresh cleansing of Your grace. Thank You for being the One True God who did not stay in the grave. Thank You for rising from the dead and ascending into heaven, making our faith different than any other. Lord, You are more powerful than we could ever know, but I pray that both my husband and I would become more aware of Your love for us and the power You possess so that our love and fear of You would grow each day. It is in Your name that I pray with thanksgiving. Amen.

Week 14

Challenge

Are you seeking God's face as you pray? As I spend time in prayer, begging God to make me a better wife, He lovingly convicts me of my need to first become a better Christian woman. I don't want to be a woman who merely attends church, prays before her meals, or participates in Bible studies; I want to be a woman who truly has a deep and vibrant *love relationship* with God and whose life is full of evidence (the "fruits" found in Galatians 5:22) that she loves Jesus with all her heart, mind, soul, and strength. True, none of us will ever be a perfect wife or Christian, but we cannot use that as an excuse to settle for mediocre.

Instead, we must pursue a deeper love relationship both with Christ and with our husbands on a daily basis. I'll admit, I don't work daily on both of these (and there are many days that I don't work on either!), despite the fact that they are the two most important relationships in my life. The truth is I can only become a better wife by loving God more. My challenge this week is to cultivate a deeper relationship with Christ and allow the fruits of the Spirit to flourish in my life so that I can better love and serve my husband.

Lord, I am humbled when I realize that my efforts to becoming a better wife are futile unless I am constantly developing a deeper walk with You. Please help me as I seek to know, love, and serve You better in order to become a more loving and selfless wife. I pray that my love relationship with You would grow and flourish deeper than before. I love you, Lord, and I pray these things in Jesus' name. Amen.

For the Love of My Husband

Father God, my prayer for my husband is that his love would abound more and more in knowledge and depth of insight, so that he might be able to discern what is best and be kept pure and blameless until You return (Philippians 1:9–10). I pray he would rejoice at Your Word as one who finds a great treasure (Psalm 119:162). Thank you, Lord, for my husband, and I pray that I would be a crown of blessing to him each day. I pray in Jesus' name. Amen.

Week 15

Challenge

I often find myself in the midst of an identity crisis: sometimes I think *I* am the Holy Spirit in Jason's life! In the past I have pointed out—sometimes in not-so-loving terms—certain areas in Jason's life where I think he could improve. As a married couple, we are called to reprove each other if needed and help hold the other accountable. However, we don't have the power to convict or stir hearts, and I shouldn't be so arrogant as to believe that God needs me to do that in my husband's life. Trying to fill the role of the Holy Spirit in his life doesn't allow Jason to be the spiritual leader of our family, and it isn't my responsibility. My challenge is to trust God to do His job while I focus on my role as a helpmate to my husband.

Father God, please forgive me for the times when I assume Your role. You don't need me to minister or convict anyone. Help me surrender my desire to control things. Allow me to focus only on my life and how I need to change instead of pointing out to my husband ways that he needs to change. I pray that Your Holy Spirit would work in his life as well as mine. I want your Spirit to teach and train me to follow You closely. In Jesus' name I pray. Amen.

For the Love of My Husband

Most High God (Daniel 7:27), I come before You humbled. I pray that You would show my husband more of Your character, more of Your nature, more of Your attributes, and more of Your majesty so that his relationship with You will grow deeper. Abba (Romans 8:15), may my husband truly know You as a daddy and declare that You are His Redeemer (Job 19:25) and Rock (Deuteronomy 32:18). May You be his Counselor (Isaiah 9:6), His King (Psalm 5:2), and his All, Lord God Almighty (Revelation 16:7). Yeshua, I pray that You continue to show Yourself to my husband so that he can know You more intimately and call You by Your many names. Show him that You truly are his Great I Am (Exodus 3:14 and John 8:58). I pray all of these things in the name of the Holy One (Acts 2:27). Amen.

Week 16

Challenge

In the book *That's Not What I Meant!* by Tim Stafford, he compares self-esteem to a table and describes the four legs that are required in order for it to stand correctly: mental, social, physical, and spiritual.[6] I enjoy building my husband up through words and actions, but I typically don't remember to focus on each of these categories. For instance, I often tell Jason how attractive he is and how I love his heart for the Lord, but I rarely commend him for his intelligence or praise the way God has wired him to interact with others. It is equally important for me to compliment his mental and social attributes as it is to recognize his physical and spiritual qualities. My challenge this week is to be more mindful of these four legs and do everything I can to boost Jason's self-esteem in a sincere and loving way.

Dear God, I pray that you would continually remind me about the four legs of self-esteem. Help me as I seek to encourage my husband in all four areas. Allow my heart and eyes to see the different mental, social, physical, and spiritual qualities You have given him. I pray that in being more mindful of these areas, You would help me fall deeper in love with my husband and the man You created him to be. In Jesus' name. Amen.

For the Love of My Husband

Precious Father, thank You so much for the gift of my husband. I ask that You protect him from any illness or disease that he may encounter. I know that sickness is a part of life, but I pray he would be a man whose body and immune system are healthy. I also pray against any terminal, chronic, or debilitating diseases that may threaten his life. If any of these are present, I ask that You would remove them as only You are capable. I pray that my husband would worship You and trust in Your promise to take away sickness (Exodus 23:25). May You always keep him physically fit, healthy, and strong so that he can be of great service to Your kingdom. I pray all of these things in Your Son's name. Amen.

Week 17

Challenge

Jason often talks about my great memory. I have the ability to recall very specific details of every date and conversation and that we have ever had. These details are usually very random and my ability to remember them always makes Jason laugh. However, I don't always apply that skill towards memorizing truly important things. Oftentimes, it is the Bible verses and inspirational quotes that I've memorized which truly make an impact in my life, so why don't I do it more often? The following quote is from Eric and Leslie Ludy's book, *The First 90 Days of Marriage*—and I *love* it! My challenge this week will be to commit this quote to memory and put it into practice:

> As the princess of the home, the wife has heavenly eyes for her man. She believes in him, she applauds his hard work, and she is his biggest fan in the world. To be a great husband, a man desperately needs a great wife. His strength and confidence hinge upon her admiration and emotional support. The more of Christ a wife shows to her husband on a daily basis, the more his impact will be upon the world each and every day. A princess of the home is both a gentle breeze and a mighty rock in her husband's life. [emphasis added] She provides refreshment, encouragement, and tenderness when her husband is weary from life's battles. And instead of nagging or manipulating when things are difficult, she offers exhortation and inspiration to motivate her man toward greatness. [7]

Precious Lord, grant me the ability and self discipline I need to not only commit this passage to memory, but also to apply it to my daily life. Please help me as I seek to show Christ to my husband every day. I pray that I will be both a gentle breeze and a mighty rock in his life. I pray that I will never nag or manipulate my husband in any way, but that I will always motivate him towards greatness. I ask these things in Jesus' mighty name. Amen.

For the Love of My Husband

Father God, it says in Your Word that as iron sharpens iron, so one man sharpens another (Proverbs 27:17). I pray that my husband would surround himself with men who will sharpen him in his faith. May he be cautious in his friendships so as to be found righteous (Proverbs 12:26). I pray that he would be able to cultivate deep relationships with other godly men who will spur him on in his walk with You and hold him accountable. Supply him with courageous friends who will boldly confront him when needed, just as Paul opposed Peter (Galatians 2:11). Grant him deep, real friendships like those of Daniel, Shadrach, Meshach, and Abednego (Daniel 1:6-17) where together they can stand up for what is right and make a difference in the world. Above all, Lord, be his best friend, and help me be the friend to him that he needs. Thank You, Jesus, that You consider us Your friends (John 15:14). I pray all of these things in the name of the One who sticks closer than a brother (Proverbs 18:24). Amen.

Week 18

Challenge

Jason and I have often talked about the need to be intentional cycle-breakers in our marriage. By that, I mean *choosing* to no longer live out the behaviors that have been prevalent in our families for years. We believe that generational curses are very real, and Satan uses them to hinder our quality of life with the bondage, judgment, shame, and anger they bring. Striving to eliminate these curses is certainly not easy, but it is necessary.

Perhaps you or your husband comes from a very unstable or broken home. If so, please focus on this week's prayer (below) and ask God to make your family one of stability, peace, and commitment. If, however, both you and your husband are fortunate enough to come from a united, godly family, I think you will still find that this prayer is applicable in your marriage. The truth is we all have problems in our families that we wish were not there. Perhaps it is a parent or grandparent who has an addiction to alcohol, pornography, gambling, or even work! Or maybe anger, lack of forgiveness, suicide, or divorce is in your family history. These curses don't necessarily have to be passed down from your parents; they may also come from close friends who have had a strong influence on your life. Whatever the case may be, as Christians in a marriage relationship, we must *choose* to be cycle-breakers from the junk in our lives. This is not only important for families with children but for *all* marriages, as we are called to be a reflection of the love between Christ and His church to a lost world. Everyone you come in contact with will benefit from your choice to break the cycle!

My challenge and prayer will go hand-in-hand this week. Since we all have different generational curses, there is not one specific prayer that would be fitting for everyone. Taking the time to make this prayer extremely raw and personal will be my challenge. I pray that Jason will be a cycle-breaker from the dysfunction of his family history, and I know that I have generational curses and dysfunction in my family that needs prayer as well. Not only do these require prayer, but also action!

For the Love of My Husband

Holy God, in the Name of Jesus Christ, I come before You today and pray for my husband and myself to break from the cycles of [insert behaviors here] that are in our lives and in our marriage. It is so easy to fall into [_____] but, Lord, we do not want these things in our marriage, and we pray that You would gouge them out! May we feel the burden to work on this daily so that we don't give in to old routines and habits that have been modeled for us. In Your Word it says that anyone who is in Christ is a new creation; the old has gone, the new has come (2 Corinthians 5:17). What a wonderful promise and, oh, how we pray that today! May we be new creations with new behaviors, ones that rest on Your truth and Your will. Use my husband and use me to break the generational curses that have been in our lives. Amen.

Week 19

Challenge

Recently, we took a family vacation to a secluded beach. It was very nice. We had sweet quality time and much laughter. Unfortunately, the weather was rotten. We were expecting sunny skies and temperatures in the 80s; instead, we saw rain all week long with highs in the 50s. Both Jason and I were disappointed as we realized that our relaxing week of lounging on the beach was not going to happen as planned. I tried to stay optimistic because I knew that Jason had planned this vacation with me in mind. However, after three days of nasty weather, I finally expressed my disappointment to Jason, and I knew he felt the same way. Of course, the time away from our normal life and being together as a family was wonderful, but we simply had to readjust our expectations for the week.

While I struggled with the disappointing weather, I prayed, "Lord, what do you want me to learn from this, specifically regarding my marriage?" The Lord was faithful in answering that prayer, but only because I asked. If we never ask God for wisdom in teachable moments, we miss out on valuable opportunities to grow in our marriage. My challenge is to develop a habit of asking God what He wants me to learn from events, stressors, and joy in my life, and then apply those lessons directly to my marriage. You might be surprised at what God has to show you.

Father God, I'm sorry for the times when I miss the lessons You are trying to teach me. Help me be a better steward of my time. When trials or joys come my way, I pray that I would be diligent about asking You what I can learn in that moment. I pray that I would be open to hearing from You in order to improve my marriage. Help me never miss a teachable moment. I love You, Jesus, and I pray this in Your name. Amen.

For the Love of My Husband

Lord, I thank You for the gifts You have given my family. Thank You that You are our Provider and that our daily needs are faithfully met. I pray that my husband would be a good steward of our money and that he would make You proud with his spending and saving habits. May he never rob You,

Lord, by forgetting or refusing to tithe (Malachi 3:8), and may he always have a generous heart toward those in need. Teach him to be a cheerful giver (2 Corinthians 9:7), and grant him financial wisdom and discipline when needed. I pray that You would use our finances for Your purpose, since all that we have is Yours already. I pray for Your blessing on my husband in all areas of his life, knowing that the blessing of the Lord makes one rich (Proverbs 10:22). In Jesus' name, I pray. Amen.

Week 20

Challenge

I really don't enjoy talking about finances. In fact, I usually avoid the topic at all costs. However, one of my friends—who isn't afraid to speak the truth in love—recently challenged me to be more supportive of Jason in this area. While I don't have any credit card debt, I am definitely a spender by nature and Jason (thankfully) is a saver. As I was talking with my friend and praying our prayer from last week, I kept thinking, "I need to sit down and speak with Jason about our budget." Believe me, this thought must have come from God because the very idea does not excite me one bit. I usually don't know (or have a *desire* to know) what our monthly bills cost, how much we are putting away for savings, or other specific details regarding our budget. Yet, I know my husband would appreciate it if I were keen to know this information and sought his opinion on my spending habits. My challenge is to initiate and participate in a budget talk with my husband, knowing that it will be important to him. The challenge for you might be a different discussion altogether. Is there a subject that you need to humbly discuss with your husband? We must take the initiative to open the lines of communication with our husbands in order to strengthen our unity.

Father God, You know and understand that there are some topics that I would be happy to never discuss with my husband, but I pray that You would help me as I have those difficult conversations with my husband in order to strengthen our marriage. Help me to be on his team and support him, not only through the conversation, but also through my actions. In Jesus' name. Amen.

For the Love of My Husband

Precious Jesus, I thank You for Your sacrifice on the cross. Thank You for being a forgiving God, gracious and compassionate, slow to anger and abounding in love (Nehemiah 9:17). I pray, Lord, that You would help my husband forgive those who have wronged him in the past. Even if he believes that he has a good reason to be mad, I pray against any bitterness that may be in his heart. I pray that he would release his anger, frustration, and hurt, and turn to You for comfort. I pray that he would feel at peace in letting these feelings go and that You would fill him with Your love and Holy Spirit. Lord, I pray that he would truly be kind and compassionate to everyone he meets, even those who have harmed him, remembering to forgive those people because You have forgiven him (Ephesians 4:32). Thank You for forgiving and loving us all, even though we hurt and betray You daily. I pray all of these things in Your name. Amen.

Week 21

Challenge

I confess that I have been slacking in my prayers for Jason. While I have been praying our focused prayers each week, I have noticed that they have been lacking in zeal. My challenge this week is simply to pray for Jason with passion. Are we really engaging in the heart of prayer? What an honor it is to pray to the Creator of the world. What an honor it is to pray for the man I love with all my heart! God has given us this incredible gift, and I never want to take for granted the privilege of kneeling before the Father on behalf of my husband's needs, actions, desires, and decisions. It is an honor to play such a vital role in our husbands' lives. I'm not sure that there is a greater or more important expression of our love than our prayers.

Dear Lord, I recommit my intentions for starting this book: please help me as I seek to pray daily for my husband. Help my prayers to be meaningful, impactful, and intentional. May I have no greater priority than praying Scripture for my husband. Thank You for listening to my prayers. In Jesus' name. Amen.

For the Love of My Husband

Father God, I pray simply that my husband would be a man of prayer. May he be joyful always, pray continually, and give You thanks in all circumstances (1 Thessalonians 5:16–18). I pray that he desires to spend time at Your feet each day in a purposeful quiet time. Allow his conversations with You to be authentic and deep. Shatter any misconception about prayer that he might have. Show him that the prayer of a righteous man is powerful and effective (James 5:16) and that You delight in and desire daily conversations with him. Thank You for giving us the honor and privilege of coming before You at any hour of the day. We love You. It is in Your Son's name we pray. Amen.

Week 22

Challenge

Earlier this week, I was frustrated with Jason, but instead of focusing on his actions, I began to pray for his prayer life. I was shocked to see how quickly my frustrations evaporated. Typically, when I am frustrated with my husband, the only prayers that I mutter are selfish in nature (e.g., "Lord, help him see things my way"). I don't think I have ever sincerely prayed *for* Jason in the midst of my frustration. This idea, praying for him and not about him, reminds me of a quote by Karol Ladd, which is going to be my challenge for this week. She says in her book, *The Power of a Positive Wife,* "Feeling frustrated with our husbands becomes an opportunity to ask God to work in their lives and in ours, conforming us to be the people we ought to be for God's glory."[8] This is so convicting, and it's really the best way to handle our frustrations. Instead of dwelling on them, we can allow God to use those moments to change us. Asking God to not only work in our husband's life, but in our own as well, will certainly allow growth and meaning to come from those challenging moments in a marriage.

Father God, I pray that I would take advantage of those moments when I am frustrated with my husband. Allow those times to be a catalyst for change in my life. Help me have an open heart toward the change You desire in me. I pray that I will take those moments of frustration and allow You to work in me, in my husband, and in my marriage. In Jesus' name, I pray. Amen.

For the Love of My Husband

Lord, I pray that my husband's attitude would be the same as that of Christ Jesus: Who, being in very nature God, did not consider equality with God something to be grasped, but made himself nothing, taking the very nature of a servant, being made in human likeness. And being found in appearance as a man, he humbled himself and became obedient to death—even death on a cross (Philippians 2:5-8). May my husband demonstrate that same humility, servant's heart, and obedience to You. I pray that he would humbly consider others better than himself, and that he would look not only to his own interests

37

but to the interests of others. Thank You, Jesus, for Your example. Encourage my husband as he seeks to be like You. It is in Your name I pray. Amen.

Week 23

Challenge

Pornography is a very uncomfortable topic, but it is one we cannot afford to ignore. A recent poll reported that 48 percent of families admit pornography is a problem in their home.[9] As I write this, I am confident that percentage has only increased.

Internet pornography, while not the only type, is a growing problem in many Christian homes because it offers easy accessibility and anonymity. Recently I heard a sermon entitled, "Keeping a Pure Mind," where the minister shared an alarming statistic that 35 percent of Christian men and 21 percent of Christian women regularly view online pornography. [10]

Pornography is a real struggle among Christians, and, though it may be awkward, we need to address it. This is not something we should sweep under the rug or act as if it doesn't impose a threat to our marriages. Open conversations between husband and wife are necessary. My challenge this week is to have an honest dialogue with my husband. This means providing a safe atmosphere for both of us to share anything we might have kept secret and to discuss ways we can fight temptations (e.g., upgrading internet filters or choosing an accountability partner).

Even if this has never been a struggle for you or your husband, you cannot assume that it never will be. Every marriage is susceptible, and we all need to be on the offense. This is especially true for Christian marriages, as we are prime targets for Satan's schemes. Many couples put boundaries in place to "affair-proof" their marriage, and in the same way, we need to be proactive in "pornography-proofing" our marriages. May God help keep all of our marriages pure!

Mighty God, I beg for Your help to keep our marriage free from pornography and lust. Lord, if there is anything unholy in my life, I pray that You would give me the resolve to remove it and seek accountability. I pray that You would enable me to have an open discussion with my husband about anything that might be in my life or in his life. Help me to be understanding and forgiving as we seek to honor You together. It is in Jesus' name that I pray. Amen.

For the Love of My Husband

Father God, with all that is in me, I cry out to You for help. Please keep my husband free from sexual immorality. You tell us to put to death our sinful nature (Colossians 3:5), which includes sexual immorality and impurity (Galatians 5:19). I pray that every day my husband will do exactly that. May there never be a hint of sexual impurity in his heart (Ephesians 3:5). I pray that You would convict him in areas that need change. May Your grace wash over him. Place a burning desire in my husband to be holy and keep our marriage bed pleasing to You (Hebrews 13:4). I pray all these things in the name of Jesus. Amen.

Week 24

Challenge

Where do you consider your home to be? Is it a certain city or street, or does your concept of home have more to do with family than location? Even though I'm currently not living there, I consider Louisville, Kentucky, my home. Lately, I've been mentioning to my husband that I would like to move back to Louisville, and yet I know that isn't a possibility, at least in the immediate future. I have noticed that I'm not doing a great job reaffirming my commitment to go (or stay) wherever he leads us. In our discussions, I talk about where I want to relocate, but I don't voice my assurance that I'll be happy wherever he is. My challenge this week is to tell my husband that *he* is my home, and I would gladly remain with him here or follow him anywhere. I will support him whether we move down the street or to another country. My husband is my home.

Lord, whether a move is in the near future for us or it is not, I pray that You would help me be committed to making my home where my husband is. Help me never to value a specific location above my own family. May my heart be at rest as long as I am with my husband. May I never allow my own desires to replace or stand in the way of what You have joined together. In Jesus' name. Amen.

For the Love of My Husband

Precious Father, I thank You for designing the covenant of marriage as You did, placing the man as the head, just as Christ is the head of the church (Ephesians 5:23). I pray for my husband to have confidence in his ability to lead our family and that he would recognize any lies from Satan that are in his life. May he know that lying is Satan's native tongue and that there is no truth in anything he says (John 8:44). I pray that my husband would take a firm stand against the devil's schemes (Ephesians 6:11) by refusing to believe them or even entertain them in his mind. I pray that he would never question his self-worth in any area of his life, but especially as the leader of our family. Fill him with Your confidence (Jeremiah 17:7) so that he can continue to make the best decisions (big or small) for our family. I pray that You would lovingly convict him when he isn't leading as You have called him to, and convict me when I'm not submitting as I'm supposed to. Please allow our marriage to be in sync with Your master design. I pray all of these things in Jesus' name. Amen.

Week 25

Challenge

A few weeks ago when our family was on vacation, the Lord taught me a powerful lesson. While we were driving through the night, Jason pulled over at 2:30 a.m. and asked if I would drive for a while because he was getting sleepy. I agreed, we hit the road, and Jason fell asleep quickly. I didn't tell him at the time, but I was freaking out. We were in the mountains of North Carolina where it was not only dark, but also very rainy. Because we had rented a car, I found myself in an SUV that I had never driven before. It was packed so full that I couldn't even see out the rear-view mirror. I was trying to navigate my way along the unfamiliar, winding roads while learning where certain controls (such as the wipers and headlights) were located on the car.

My knuckles were white as my eyes darted from the side mirrors, to the road, to the GPS, and then to my family. I think a large part of my fear was the fact that my beloved husband, precious daughter, and wonderful little dog were all sleeping peacefully in the car. I felt so much stress and pressure knowing that their safety— indeed, their very lives—were in my hands. Each decision I made, each turn I took, led my family somewhere, and I prayed that I wouldn't make any costly mistakes. While talking to Jesus along the road, I heard Him speak into my heart. He shared with me that what I was experiencing at that moment is what Jason experiences all the time as the leader of our home. *Wow!* I contemplated that for several days, and then finally asked Jason if that truly is how he feels. His response was an immediate, "Yes, all the time. Constantly."

His response was quite sobering for me. You see, if I were asked, I would admit that I view myself as dancing through life. And while I may have stressful times and feel outside pressures, it certainly isn't a continual burden, and it is nothing in comparison to the weight of knowing that the well-being of my entire family rests on my shoulders. My challenge is to remember that valuable experience and do whatever I can to help Jason carry the weight. Since he is the provider and protector of the family, I can't remove all the pressure from him. I can, however, come alongside him and serve as his partner, ready to help him in whatever capacity he needs, using my words to build him up and thank him for all he does.

Precious Lord, I pray that my eyes would be open to the pressures that my husband experiences on a daily basis. Encourage me to support him in whatever capacity he needs. I pray that I would never make his job as provider and protector harder than it already is, but that I would be mindful of his sense of responsibility and look for ways to build him up. In Jesus' name I pray. Amen.

For the Love of My Husband

Father God, in the book of Deuteronomy, You told Moses to encourage Joshua so that he would be able to lead the Israelites into the Promised Land. In the same way that You called Moses to speak into Joshua's life, I pray that You would bring someone into my husband's life who would encourage and strengthen him to do great things. You tell us several times in Your Word that we are to encourage each other daily (Hebrews 3:13, 1 Thessalonians 5:11), and I pray that You would use me and others to encourage my husband and speak truth into his life. I pray that he will receive affirmation from several different people, praising him for the job he is doing in both his family life and in his career. May my husband always strive to please You and receive Your affirmation. In Jesus' name, I pray. Amen.

Week 26

Challenge

The producers of the Christian movie *Fireproof* were very purposeful in casting actors who walked closely with the Lord. I had the opportunity to see Erin Bethea speak, and she said that, during auditions, the potential actors were was asked if there was anything in their lives that might cause God to take His hand of blessing off of the movie if they were offered a role.[11] That is a serious question that requires humility, honesty, and time to answer. While we do serve a compassionate God who loves us fiercely and unconditionally despite all of our sins, He desires for us to live God-honoring lives. Indeed, there may be times when He removes His hand of blessing from us because of sin in our life that needs to be addressed.

I was thinking about that question this week and how I should continually apply it to every ministry in my life. There is no ministry greater than my marriage, so I rewrote the question to look like this: *Is there anything in my life, right now, at this moment, that could cause God to take His hand of blessing off my marriage?* I certainly don't want the Lord to ever remove His hand of blessing from my marriage because of sin in my life. My challenge is to contemplate and pray through this question and to take action as the Lord prompts.

Father God, I pray that You would show me areas in my life that are unpleasing to You. Help me to make things right with You so that Your hand of blessing will remain on my marriage. I pray that I would never think too highly of myself as a Christian or as a wife. Thank You for Your forgiveness, and I pray these things in the name of Jesus. Amen.

For the Love of My Husband

Lord, keep my husband from willful sins; may they not rule over him. I pray he will be blameless and innocent of great transgression. May the words of his mouth and the meditation of his heart be pleasing in Your sight, O Lord, my Rock and my Redeemer (Psalm 19:13-14). In Jesus' name. Amen.

Week 27

Challenge

I recently realized that there are certain sins in my life that don't bother me as much as they should. While I know that a certain attitude or action is wrong, I'm not always spurred to repent. As I was reflecting on last week's challenge, the Lord spoke clearly into my spirit and said, "If you only knew how much your sin breaks My heart." In response to the Lord, I asked Him to give me a heart like His.

That has been a dangerous prayer, because not only am I now grieved about the sin in my life, but I am also moved to pray earnestly for the salvation of those close to me and even those I pass on the street. I have only scratched the surface so far, but I am slowly realizing how deeply moved the Lord is for each one of us. He cares about every aspect and detail of our lives. Saying, "Jesus loves you!" is so easy, but it takes more effort to truly comprehend that the Lord is aware of the comings and goings of every person on earth. He is pursuing them relentlessly, loving them unconditionally, crying with them, and longing to comfort them. His Heart is so tender! My challenge this week is to apply these qualities I'm learning about God toward loving my husband in a more tender and pure way.

Father God, thank You for the Holy Spirit and the conviction that comes through Him. I pray that I would take the sin in my life seriously and use that as motivation to repent. In addition, Lord, I pray that You would help me as I seek to understand Your heart in a deeper way. Help me to better understand how tender and loving Your heart is, and make my heart more like yours. Please help me be more loving and tender with my husband. Allow me to care deeply and passionately about his comings and goings, his walk with You, and every detail of his life. In Jesus' loving name I pray. Amen.

For the Love of My Husband

Loving Father, use my husband to bring Your love into the lives of those around him. Heal his heart and make it clean. Open up his eyes to the things unseen. Show him how to love like You have loved him. Please break his heart for what breaks Yours. [12] May he be compassionate and gracious, slow to anger, and abounding in love, just as You are (Psalm 103:8). In Jesus' name. Amen.

Week 28

Challenge

Typically, my day begins whenever my daughter, Havana, wakes and I hear her talking through the baby monitor. Then, I sluggishly roll out of bed, get her dressed, fix breakfast, and begin my daily routine of household chores and taking care of my family. Needless to say, it takes me at least an hour to feel like I'm fully functioning. I'm simply not a morning person. In her book *Becoming the Woman God Wants Me to Be,* Donna Partow encourages the reader to prioritize quiet time and make it the very first activity of each day:

> If you want to be an inspiration to everyone you meet, meet with God first. ... Every book and biography I've ever read by spiritual leaders, past and present, and every person ever used mightily of God indicated that meeting with God was their first order of business. Morning devotions set the agenda and the tone for the day.[13]

I don't know about you, but this is not a habit I have mastered. Instead, I typically wait until I have a free moment later in the day to spend time with God (which often never comes!). The more I have thought about the above paragraph, the more I am convinced of its truth. My challenge this week is to wake up before the rest of my family in order to spend time alone with God in His Word. Starting the day with a purposeful quiet time can only enhance my efforts to become a better wife.

Father God, I am sorry for the times when I put other things before spending time with You and time in Your Word. I pray that I would develop the self-discipline to wake up before anyone else in my house in order to spend ample time at Your feet. Help me learn to protect that time and to not let sleep or chores prevent me from meeting with you. Continue to impress upon my heart the importance of this private time together so that I might grow as a woman and wife. I love You, Jesus, and pray these things in Your name. Amen.

For the Love of My Husband

Sweet and Mighty Father, I pray that my husband would fall deeper in love with You through Your Word. I pray that the powerful truths You have given us will be hidden in his heart so that he may use them to ward off Satan's temptations just as Jesus did while living on this earth (Psalm 119:11, Matthew 4:1–11). I pray that he would view the Bible as a lamp to his feet and a light for his path (Psalm 119:105). Please help my husband develop such a strong hunger for Your Word that he is willing to sacrifice sleep in order to grow in Your truths. May Your Words teach him, rebuke him, correct him, and train him in righteousness (2 Timothy 3:16), for we know that they are living and active and sharper than any double-edged sword. May that sword penetrate even the deepest, darkest places of my husband's heart (Hebrews 4:12). Meet him where he is, and may he cherish each moment he has in Your Word and then crave more. Lovingly convict him when he isn't reading or obeying Scripture as he should. In the name of Jesus, I pray. Amen.

Week 29

Challenge

Does your marriage have synergy? The concept of synergy involves the interaction of two parts that when combined; produce a total effect that is greater than the sum of the individual efforts. In other words, with synergy, two plus two equals greater than four. Examples of synergy are abundant all around us, especially in nature. For instance, have you ever wondered why a flock of geese fly in a "V" formation? The answer is synergy! Science has proven that when flying together, geese can move much faster and travel greater distances than any one goose can accomplish when flying alone. The geese in the front of the formation create an uplift pattern of air flow which allows the geese in the back to work less strenuously. As the lead geese become tired, they rotate to the rear to benefit from the synergy phenomenon.

King Solomon suggests this same principle in Ecclesiastes 4:9 by saying, "Two are better than one because they have a good return for their work." So how can we apply this concept of synergy to our marriages? Well, our husbands need us to partner with them in order to achieve certain goals. For example, if you are a working wife and your salary, either part or whole is considered "yours" to spend however you wish, you may be missing an opportunity to combine your income with your husband's in order to reach your financial goals more quickly. Also, if your husband is trying to live a healthy lifestyle, perhaps you could join him in dieting and exercising regularly so that you may encourage and motivate one another. Finally, if you and your husband are involved in separate ministries, consider combining your talents in unity to produce an even greater harvest for the Kingdom of God. You may be surprised with the end result when you partner with your husband.

My challenge is to become more synergistic in my marriage. I must use my talents and gifts to complement Jason's efforts as he leads our family. This will require an open discussion of our long term goals and a willing spirit on my behalf.

Father God, please help my husband and me have synergy. Allow the work of our hands to produce a harvest far greater than we could produce on our own. I pray that our efforts would be combined in every way so that we can be most productive. Please forgive me when my own selfish wants or desires stand in the way of combining with my husband. In Jesus' name, I pray. Amen.

For the Love of My Husband

Lord, thank You for the gift of marriage and for my wonderful husband, whom I love. In Your Word, You say that many men claim to have unfailing love, but a faithful man is hard to find (Proverbs 20:6). Father, I pray that my husband would be a faithful man to both You and me. I pray that he would take his marriage vows very seriously. Give my husband a strong desire to cultivate our relationship as a sign of his loyalty and commitment to our marriage. I pray that his heart would be pure and never divided in his commitment to me. In Jesus' name, I ask for my husband to be a man of strong integrity, and I pray that he will never compromise any of his convictions and commitments. I pray for Your grace, strength, and resolve to help us continually choose to be a couple that is only separated by death. In Jesus' name, I pray. Amen.

Week 30

Challenge

Sometimes I struggle with being content, and I'll bet I'm not alone. Based on books I've read and conversations I've had with other women, contentment is something that almost all of us have had to deal with at one time or another. Do any of these sound familiar?

- I'll be happy when I'm married.

- My life will be perfect when I have children.

- If only we lived in a bigger house.

- I want to take a vacation to Hawaii like they did.

- I wish I had a different job.

- I hate my weight.

- My life would be better if my husband was more like her husband.

Have you ever played this comparison game? I have! I find myself wishing for a nicer house, car, or clothes. I often compare myself to others when it comes to looks, and lately I've been playing the comparison game when it comes to children. Jason and I struggled with infertility for three years, during which we experienced a miscarriage and a failed adoption. Since Havana's birth, things have continued to be rocky, as we've been trying unsuccessfully to conceive for months. I have experienced so many emotions during our journey, and while those emotions are normal, the sheer envy I struggle with is not appropriate. The Lord is calling me to release my envy to Him, which will not only make a good topic for my challenge but an appropriate theme for our prayer.

I strongly believe that lack of contentment in a marriage has the potential to become toxic, even if your comparisons are not directly related to your spouse. If you find yourself easily dissatisfied with your life in general and think (even just subconsciously) that a new job, husband, baby, or home will magically make your life better, then I suggest you spend time in prayer and seek a deeper relationship with Christ, as He is the only thing that can truly satisfy. Ask yourself, what aspect of your life are you not content with? What can *you* do about it? If you aren't content in your marriage, then what can *you* do to fix it? Notice that I did not ask what your *husband* can do. If you are struggling with materialism, what void are you trying to fill with stuff? If you are not content with your appearance despite living a healthy lifestyle, perhaps you can focus on what the Bible defines as true beauty. For me, my challenge this week is to choose to believe that my happiness will not depend on my ability to become pregnant and I will stop comparing myself to other, more fertile women.

Certainly, being content does not mean that life is picture perfect and we are walking around on cloud nine all the time. We live in a fallen world, and we have struggles, trials, and physical ailments, and, unfortunately, we lose people we love. Life is hard. However, we can still choose to be content with our lives and all of our circumstances, even if they grieve us. Let us resolve not to allow discontentment to grow in our hearts, choosing never to say, "I'll be happy when ..."

Father God, it is impossible to find contentment outside of You, yet I know I seek it in so many other places. Please convict me when my heart tries to find happiness apart from You. Please help me be a woman who is content with every area of her life. I pray that I would never compare my husband to any other man and that I would love and support him for who he is. Thank You, Lord, for being the only true source of contentment. In Jesus' name. Amen.

For the Love of My Husband

Lord, thank You for being our only true source of contentment. I pray that my husband would never seek fulfillment in material possessions or career success but always be content with what he has, trusting that You will never leave or forsake him (Hebrews 13:5). I pray my husband would be like Paul and say that he has learned the secret of being content in any and every situation (Philippians 4:12). Help my husband to serve and obey You alone, so that he may spend the rest of his days in contentment (Job 36:11). I look forward to seeing Your work in my husband's life. It is in Your Son's Name that I pray. Amen.

Week 31

Challenge

The Bible has many different translations. Sometimes reading a familiar verse in a new version can bring a fresh perspective to the Word. I recently read Song of Solomon 3:4 in the New American Standard Version, which reads, "Scarcely had I left them when I found him whom my soul loves; I held on to him and would not let him go until I had brought him to my mother's house, and into the room of her who conceived me."

I was moved by the middle of that verse where it says, "I found him whom my soul loves. I held onto him and would not let him go." How powerful! I have found the one my soul loves, and throughout the rest of my life—the ups and downs, for better or for worse—I want it to be ingrained in my heart and head that I am to hold onto him and not let him go. My challenge is to memorize that version of the verse and apply it daily to my marriage. Physically and emotionally, I am holding on to Jason and—come what may—I will not let him go. It will be a reminder of our firm decision that divorce or affairs are never, ever an option in marriage.

Lord, thank You for Your Word. I pray that You would help me as I seek to memorize this passage of Scripture. Help me to apply it to my attitude and actions, that no matter what may come, Lord, I am holding on to the one my soul loves and I will not let him go. That is a choice only I can make and so I pray that You would empower me to never let go, emotionally or physically, to my husband. In Jesus' name, I pray. Amen.

For the Love of My Husband

Father God, I pray that in view of Your mercy in his life, my husband would offer his body as a living sacrifice, holy and pleasing to You, as his spiritual act of worship. I pray that he will no longer conform to the pattern of this world, but that he would be transformed by the renewing of his mind. I pray he will be able to test and approve what Your will is—Your good, pleasing, and perfect will for his life (Romans 12:1-2). Thank You for the plan You have had for him since the beginning of time. May he be faithful to Your calling. In Your Son's name, I pray. Amen.

Week 32

Challenge

God has been showing me that I am not as flexible as I thought I was. I used to pride myself in being a "go with the flow" type of girl. I'm beginning to realize, however, that I'm only a "go with the flow" person when *I'm* controlling the flow. There has been more than one occasion in the past when Jason has expressed that he needs me to be more flexible. Usually my responses to him have been filled with sarcasm and resistance. How embarrassing. I would like to think that I have improved in this quality over time, but I know there are times that I still struggle with flexibility.

We went out of town for a few days this past week and the night before we left, I realized that we would arrive at our destination around 8 a.m., but couldn't check into the hotel until 3 p.m. My first response was to freak out. What would I do with a nine-month-old baby for almost seven hours? How would she get her morning nap? What would she eat for breakfast and lunch? How would I keep her entertained? Before I was able to express my anxiety, though, God grabbed a hold of my heart and impressed upon me that I needed to be flexible. He would work out the details even if it wasn't our normal routine. Amazingly, it was one of the sweetest days we have ever had as a family! I noticed that my flexibility helped the tone of our whole day to be relaxed and fun. It reminded me that the wife truly does set the tone for the household.

How many times have I been unnecessarily uptight and made Jason feel tense in his home? Proverbs 31:12 says that a wife of noble character "brings her husband *good, not harm,* all the days of his life." One way in which I can bring good to my husband is by setting a comfortable tone in the house. How much nicer would our vacations, days off, and evenings at home be if I would simply relax? That is my challenge this week, and perhaps it is applicable to you, too. Are there ways you can be more flexible? Or is the opposite true in your case? Perhaps you are too relaxed in some areas and need to set a more structured tone for your home. Talk to your husband about it. Ask what you can do to make the atmosphere of your home one in which he feels loved, replenished, and peaceful.

Father God, sometimes I forget the responsibility that I have as a wife to impact the tone of the household. I pray, Lord, that You would help me support my husband and develop a tone that is best for our family. Please help me not to be too flexible or too rigid. I pray that I will bring my husband good, and not harm, all the days of his life. I pray these things in the name of Jesus. Amen.

For the Love of My Husband

Dear Lord, thank You for always being present in our lives. You are the only constant in our ever-changing world, and for that we praise You. It brings me great comfort that You don't change like the shifting shadows (James 1:17), but Your love for us will always remain. I pray that my husband would know Your love for him more intimately than he's ever known it before, and that he would trust in Your unfailing love forever and ever (Psalm 52:8). I pray that he would experience the absolute joy, even to the point of tears, of knowing that You are in his heart (Galatians 4:6). I pray he is secure in the promise that You will never leave him (John 14:18), and that he can count on You no matter how lonely he might feel. I pray that my husband would not forget that You are always with him (Matthew 28:20). May that truth cut through all the noise, pain, worry, and anxiety he might allow into his heart. It is in Your Son's precious name I pray. Amen.

Week 33

Challenge

SEX.

It is impossible to pray daily for our husbands and challenge ourselves as wives without discussing the topic of sex. I firmly believe that part of a wife's ministry to her husband is sexual in nature. I think Jason and I have the best love life in the history of the world, but that has not always been the case. In the past, this topic was at the root of many of our fights. At times, it even caused a lot of stress and tension in our home. This should not be! God never intended for sex to be a source of contention, but an incredible gift. Within the context of biblical marriage, sex is beautiful, holy, and fun. It is a foretaste of heaven, a renewal of our wedding vows, and a form of worship. It is never supposed to be boring, cause one to feel ashamed, or create arguments.

In conversations I've had with other women, many wives express that they wish their husbands would "leave them alone," and they speak of the drudgery of sex. Some say this is because "men are microwaves and women are slow cookers," and if the man hasn't allowed the woman to warm up slowly and properly, then she'll not be in the mood. Have you heard that analogy? Does that describe you? If it does, let me encourage you, as your challenge this week, to make an effort to help yourself get in the mood. For some, that might be lighting candles, thinking positive thoughts about your husband during the day, or buying lingerie. For others it might be reading old love letters from your husband or making sure the kitchen is clean before going to bed so you aren't distracted with any household chores or other responsibilities.

The slow cooker analogy does not apply to me, and that has been a source of frustration. I struggled with the fact that I wasn't like the stereotypical woman. In fact, I didn't know many women like me at all, so I often felt ashamed or like something was wrong with me because I enjoyed sex. Finally, I had to shrug off everything I'd read in books or heard at conferences about all women being slow cookers and embrace being the microwave that I am. Since doing that, our love life has been much better.

So, if you enjoy sex, please, know you are *not* alone—God has designed you that way! Sex became much less stressful once I embraced that idea. It was ingrained in my mind that the man should always initiate sex, which isn't true at all. For a microwave, that can be very frustrating. Therefore, if you are like me, perhaps our challenge might be to stop feeling embarrassed and to start being more comfortable with initiating sex.

So, whether you are a slow cooker or a microwave, embrace the identity God has given you. Don't be afraid to discuss your sex life with your spouse on a regular basis, making sure both of your needs are being met. Please realize that the frequency of sex depends on our spouses' needs, not ours alone. Is there some agreement you and your husband need to reach? Are his needs being met? Are yours? Is sex fun? Work together, discuss, and enjoy! God has incredible plans for your sex life; are you living up to them?

For the Love of My Husband

Father God, thank You for the gift of sex! Thank You for creating us with the ability to love each other and worship You through physical intimacy. I pray that You will help me find creative ways to love my husband. May I always be able to meet his needs, please him, and be desirable to him (Song of Solomon 7:10). Make us eager to fulfill our marital duties to each other (1 Corinthians 7:3) as a sign of our faithful love. I pray that my husband would always be satisfied with me (Proverbs 5:18) and that our sexual intimacy would be fresh, positive, and selfless in nature. Bless my husband's sexuality and make it an area of fulfillment in his life. Protect us from apathy, disappointment, criticism, busyness, resentment, or disinterest in the bedroom. I pray that neither of us will ever be tempted to think about seeking fulfillment elsewhere. I commit this area of our lives to You, Lord; may it be continually new and alive. I pray for an incredible love life—better than we've ever known or could ever expect. Make it all that You created it to be. In Jesus' name, I pray. Amen.

Week 34

Challenge

Sometimes I forget to pray for Jason throughout the day. I'm great at praying for him during my devotion time and before going to bed at night, but in the hustle and bustle of the day, my prayer life often goes by the wayside. My challenge this week is to remind myself to lift my husband up in prayer during the day. Here is one creative tip that I recently heard: Set your phone alarm for specific times throughout the day to remind yourself to pray. For example, I will be setting my phone alarm for 12:19 p.m. and 4:12 p.m. every day. The 12:19 alarm represents our anniversary date, when I'll say a quick prayer for our marriage, and 4:12 is for Jason's birthday, to pray specifically for him. No matter where I am or who I am with, I can say a silent prayer each day at those times. With this new method, I'm hoping that I can become more disciplined about praying for Jason and our marriage throughout the day.

Lord, as simple as it sounds, thank You for alarm clocks. Help me as I set a few each day to remind myself to specifically pray for my husband and our marriage. Please continue to prompt me to pray daily for my husband. I love You, Jesus, and I ask this in Your name. Amen.

For the Love of My Husband

Father God, I pray that my husband would set his heart on things above and not on earthly things. Help him put to death whatever belongs to his earthly nature: sexual immorality, impurity, lust, evil desires, and greed. May he be diligent in ridding himself of all anger, rage, malice, and slander and removing filthy language from his lips. I pray that he would not lie to anyone, since he has taken off his old self with its practices and has put on his new self, which is being renewed in the knowledge of Your image. May my husband clothe himself with compassion, kindness, humility, gentleness, and patience. And over all these virtues, may he put on love, which binds them all together in perfect unity. I pray for the peace of Christ to rule in his heart. May he let the word of Christ dwell in him richly as he teaches and admonishes others with all wisdom, and as he sings psalms, hymns, and spiritual songs with gratitude in his heart to You. Whatever he does, whether in word or deed, may he do it all in the name of the Lord Jesus, giving thanks to You, the Father through Him. Amen. (Colossians 3:1–17)

Week 35

Challenge

Have you ever participated in a spiritual retreat? I love the unique benefits of spiritual retreats. They foster individual time with God, encourage spiritual growth, and provide a refreshing atmosphere in which the participant may focus more clearly on Christ.

Many of us would claim that we attempt to have some form of a quiet time regularly. Most of us would also say that we try to attend a church service at least once a week. But in the demanding tasks of each and every day how many of us can say that we actively carve out time to participate in a spiritual retreat? I know that I can't claim that. In fact, it is hard for me to remember the last retreat I actually attended. Oftentimes it is our daily responsibilities and our very desire to be the best wife possible that prevents us from sitting down and simply being still at the feet of our Lord which is something we are commanded to do in Psalm 46:10 and Luke 10:42.

My challenge, then, is to dedicate at least an hour this week where I can commit to spiritual replenishment and personal renewal at the feet of Jesus. This might be through a structured retreat or simply a visit to the sanctuary at my church while sitting down with my Bible, a pen, and some paper. I will use that time to pray, listen, and recommit my life and my marriage to the Lord. In addition to my mini-retreat, I will also sit down with my husband and commit to a time when we can participate in something for our marriage. This might be an upcoming retreat, an educational class, or simply a Sunday school group for couples. We must be aggressive about seeking out and protecting those moments of escape that the Lord provides through spiritual retreats.

Dear Lord, You have a deep desire for us to simply be still and sit at Your feet. I am sorry for the times when I neglect that priority. Please help me this week to find and protect time where I simply sit at Your feet in a unique and refreshing setting. Help me to focus on You and listen to Your voice. In Jesus' name I pray. Amen.

For the Love of My Husband

Father God, please forgive me when I don't take the responsibility to pray for my husband seriously enough. Lord, I pray that You would do mighty works in my husband in ways that neither one of us can imagine. Through the joys, trials, fears, and achievements in his life, may he allow You to use those things to shape him, mold him, correct him, and bring him closer to You. In Your Son's name, I pray. Amen.

Week 36

Challenge

Most people wouldn't know it, but I tend to be a worrier by nature. It seems like worrying has become something that I struggle with a little more every year, and I must admit that I've been struggling with it a lot recently. You may remember from a previous devotion the unfortunate miscarriage and failed adoption that Jason and I have experienced. Well, we recently learned that we are pregnant again, and while this is exciting news, it also invokes tremendous fear in my heart. Honestly, I am very scared that I will lose another child, and I'm not sure how well I can handle another loss. Each moment of the day, I wrestle with fear, wondering whether this new little life will survive in my womb. My anxiety has become so great that it has brought tension into my marriage. The only thing I have talked about recently is my fear of losing our baby, and Jason finally brought it to my attention that I need to have more faith and trust in God instead of being consumed with worry.

Now, I can easily list several verses from the Bible that speak on the topic of fear (Philippians 4:6, 2 Timothy 1:7, etc.) but that does little good unless I apply those principles to my attitude, claim them in my life, and use them to combat the Devil. As I have said before, maturing in my relationship with God is the catalyst that will ultimately make the biggest difference in my attitude and actions as a wife. Therefore, my challenge this week is to grow deeper in my understanding of God's prescription for fear and claim His Biblical truths in my life. It is never God's plan for fear to drive a wedge between husband and wife. Let us resolve, then, to be wives of faith, not wives of worry.

Lord, how trivial our worry must seem to You at times! I'm so grateful that You have many prescriptions for fear in the Bible. I pray that I would take each one to heart and claim them in my life. Help me to overcome my fear and allow it to draw me close to You and bring me back to Your Word. In Jesus' name, I pray. Amen.

For the Love of My Husband

Father God, I thank You for the many promises found in the Bible. I pray that my husband would know Your Word so intimately that he would be able to proclaim Your Scriptural Truths in his life whenever he is tempted or discouraged. Teach my husband to hide Your Word in his heart so that he might not sin against You (Psalms 119:11). May he meditate on Your precepts and find delight in Your decrees (Psalm 119:15-16). Lord, You promise that Your words will accomplish what You desire, and I pray that Your powerful Word would not return void in my husband's life (Isaiah 55: 11). Help him to cling to the Truth no matter what circumstances he may face. Thank You for being faithful and true. We love You, Jesus, and it is in Your Name that I pray. Amen.

Week 37

Challenge

Do you respect your husband? I love and respect Jason with my whole heart, and my respect for him has only increased over the years. While I often tell Jason how much I love him, I don't always express my respect for him with the same regularity. I am learning, however, that men need to feel respected even more than they need to feel loved. A must-read for every married couple is *Love and Respect* by Dr. Emerson Eggerichs. Of all the marriage books Jason and I have read together, that one is *his* favorite. I have taken some cues from Dr. Eggerichs and begun to focus on Jason's need for respect in our marriage, but I am only beginning to truly understand the magnitude of this need. Therefore, my challenge this week is to express my respect for him daily. Every time I tell him that I love him I will also add the words, "I respect you." In verbally confirming my respect for him, I aim to keep God's command in Ephesians 5:33: "However, each one of you also must love his wife as he loves himself, and the wife must respect her husband."

Lord, I know You tell us in Your Word that we are to respect our husband. That is not something we should overlook. Please help me as I seek to communicate to my husband, not only my love for him, but also my respect. In Jesus' name. Amen.

For the Love of My Husband

Father God, I thank You for Your Word and the truth that it contains. I thank You that my husband knows, follows, and loves You. I pray, Lord, in the name of Jesus, that he will never be led astray and that his heart would be steadfast with love and dedication to You alone. I pray that he will learn more about Your Word daily so that he can recognize false gospels (Galatians 1:6), and I pray that he would teach others how to have wisdom in this area as well. Holy Spirit, give him insight into what is true and what is false so that he won't be thrown into confusion by people trying to pervert the gospel (Galatians 1:7). I pray, Lord, that he will never desert You. May he daily cling to the grace offered solely through Jesus Christ, and may he always be confident in the message of the Gospel, knowing that it is not invented by any man (Galatians 1:11–12). I pray that my husband will never forsake You, his first love (Revelation 2:4). And when that love goes through trials, I pray that he remains faithful, confident, and devoted to You. I pray all of these things in Your Son's powerful name. Amen.

Week 38

Challenge

As a follow up to last week's devotion, I want to dig deeper in the concept of respecting our husbands. Last week's challenge was to express our respect on a daily basis, but I am learning that it is not quite that simple. We know that we are instructed to respect, but what does that actually look like in a marriage? What does that mean to the man you married?

I asked Jason a few years ago what I could do to show him respect. He answered with, "Trust me." At first I didn't understand what he meant, so he clarified with an example. You see, I usually stop to fuel up my car whenever the gauge is at the one-quarter mark. I have always done so, and I am proud to say that I have never run out of gas. Jason, on the other hand, will drive the car until it is very close to empty. In fact, the gauge can even be *past* the "E," and he is still confident that we can make it home (to his credit, he has never run out of gas either). He said that when we are driving together and I suggest that we need to stop to buy gas, he feels I do not trust him to take care of the situation. I was very thankful for the example because I had never considered that my suggestion to buy gas would be considered disrespectful to him. Since then, I have done my best to keep that in mind when we travel together.

Last week, as I was focusing on our challenge, I noticed some other habits that do not communicate respect to my husband. For instance, sometimes when I am getting dressed, I ask Jason which shirt I should wear, but I don't always choose the one he suggests. Likewise, I have been known to ask him if my hair looks good in a certain style, and when he says, "Yes," I often respond with, "Are you sure?" If I want to communicate that I truly respect his opinion, then I need to listen to and follow his suggestions. Similarly, I should trust him when he says my hair looks nice. If I'm going to change my outfit or hair no matter what he thinks, then I really shouldn't ask his opinion at all. When he gives me his opinion on something, I should receive it without hesitation. Even if I don't intend to communicate a message of disrespect, what really matters is how my husband perceives my actions, words, and habits.

My challenge is to be a wife who *tells* her husband that she respects him and a wife that consistently *shows* her husband that she respects him! I will ask Jason for more examples of how I can show him respect and pray for the Holy Spirit to prompt me in these areas that need change.

Father God, respect is easy to say, but a lot harder to show. I pray that You would help me as I seek to show my husband my respect for him. Teach me what it means to be respectful and help me apply it to my marriage. I pray that my actions would demonstrate my unwavering respect and that I would take my husband's need for respect seriously. Grant me a respectful spirit, Lord, so that I may bless my husband. In Jesus' name. Amen.

For the Love of My Husband

Precious Jesus, thank You for being a God of compassion. Throughout the Gospels, it says that You were "filled with compassion" for the hurting people You saw all around You. Lord, You are the same yesterday, today, and forever (Hebrews 13:8). I pray that my husband would know that You are filled with compassion for him in every area of his life. Whether it is a certain sin in his life that he desperately wants to conquer or an illness or heartache that he may be facing, please meet him where he is and may he accept the compassion that You offer. I pray that he comes to know Your compassionate nature intimately, Lord. While doing so, I pray that You will challenge him to be a man who is filled with Christ-like compassion for others, showing compassion to everyone in Your name and coming alongside them in whatever struggle they might experience. Help his understanding of Your compassion make him a greater light in this dark world. It is in Your loving and compassionate name I pray. Amen.

Week 39

Challenge

Sadly, today's culture encourages couples to live together before marriage, women to bash their husbands, and men to distance themselves from their families. It is no wonder that the divorce rate in America is nearly 50 percent! God's Biblical plan for marriage, however, is drastically different than the trends our culture has produced. What can we as wives do to become more countercultural?

For starters, we must be loving, submitting, honoring, respecting, and cherishing our husbands, not based on what he does, but out of our own obedience to Christ. We can make a choice to speak highly of our husbands and passionately about the sacred institution of marriage, even when it is not popular to express those views. Author and speaker Matthew Kelly says, "If enough of us are countercultural, then a new culture will emerge."[14] Let our challenge this week be working together to create a new culture where wives gladly submit to their husbands and where marriage is not only valued but lasts a lifetime!

Dear Lord, I pray that you would help me be a countercultural wife. I pray that I would be committed to love, submit to, honor, respect, and cherish my husband—even when I don't feel like it. May I only speak positively to and about him, and may we represent marriage well. Thank You for Your design for marriage; I pray that I never mistake the world's normal for Your best. In Jesus' name, I pray. Amen.

For the Love of My Husband

"There is a stunning, tragic, sinful, visible lack of testosterone in American evangelicalism, and we are afraid to admit it." – Albert Mohler, President of the Southern Baptist Theological Seminary[15]

Father God, I pray in the name of Jesus Christ that my husband will not be part of the lack of testosterone in American evangelicalism. I pray that You would enable him to speak Your Word with great boldness (Acts 4:29) each day. In all his comings and goings, and with everyone he meets, I pray that he will acknowledge You before all men (Matthew 10:32). Lord, I pray that he would not compromise the truth, but rather that he would be like Daniel and always stand up for what is right (Daniel 6). Jesus, I pray that You would give him more of Your heart for the lost, both in America and abroad. May my husband be like Jeremiah, with Your Word burning in his heart like a fire shut up in his bones that he cannot hold in (Jeremiah 20:9). Cause my husband to be a contagious Christian! Amen.

Week 40

Challenge

I have been introduced to a prayer called the "Prayer of Indifference." The concept is praying to be indifferent toward anything except the will of God. I don't know about you, but that idea steps all over my toes; I am often guilty of having an agenda when it comes to my own life. Ruth Haley Barton describes this principle in her book, *Strengthening the Soul of Your Leadership*:

> We need to also pray for indifference. This is not the kind of indifference that we associate with apathy; rather, it is the prayer that we would be indifferent to everything but the will of God. ... As Danny Morris and Charles Olsen put it: "God's will, nothing more, nothing less, nothing else." The prayer for indifference can be a very challenging prayer for us to pray, because most times we enter into decision-making with strong opinions and more than a little self-interest. It takes time, and often a death to self is required before we can see God's will taking shape in our lives. Here we ask ourselves the question, what needs to die in me in order for the will of God to come forth in and among us?[16]

Personally, I find it is easy to say that I want God's will for my life. In reality, whenever His will isn't parallel with mine, I am not so eager to follow it. I have noticed that my need for control often prevents me from truly welcoming His plan. My challenge, then, is to honestly evaluate what aspects of my life need to die in order for the will of God to triumph in my life and in my marriage. The challenge doesn't stop there; it continues with me putting those obstacles to death. I'm waiting with great anticipation to see what God's will truly holds for our lives when we pray for indifference.

Lord, what in me needs to die in order for Your will to triumph in my life and in my marriage? I know Your answer won't be an easy one, but I am open to hearing and acting upon Your guidance. I pray that You would help me embrace this idea of being indifferent to anything outside of Your will. Please make my will a reflection of Your own. In Jesus' name. Amen.

For the Love of My Husband

Father God, You say in Your Word that You give Your followers the desires of their hearts (Psalm 37:4). Lord, I pray that You would also give my husband the desires of Your heart. I pray that he would truly be indifferent to everything except for Your good and perfect will (Romans 12:2), even when it doesn't line up with his own wishes. May his life and family truly reflect Your will, nothing more, nothing less, nothing else. Please enable him to deny himself daily (Luke 9:23) in order to understand You better. May having the attitude of indifference be the only desire of his heart. It is in Your Son's name I pray. Amen.

Week 41

Challenge

This past week I closely observed Jason, and I noticed that he went above and beyond in demonstrating his love for me many times. For example, Monday was our "dating anniversary" (the anniversary of our first date). I know he doesn't feel the need to celebrate this occasion now that we are married, but he knows that I enjoy it, so he humors me. This year he brought me breakfast in bed, planned a romantic dinner, and bought me several gifts including cookies from my favorite bakery. By the end of the night, I felt very loved, and I was blown away by all the time he had invested in an event that is much more important to me than it is to him. Indeed, I thought he went above and beyond. While his behavior this week may not be all that different from any other week, it was the first time I truly realized all that he does for me. His actions have led me to my newest challenge: I want to go above and beyond for Jason!

Going above and beyond may seem like a vague concept. Honestly, that is because it will look different in each marriage. For me personally, I can go above and beyond for Jason by making the time to clean out my car and get it more organized. Doing that without being asked would definitely bless Jason, as he often drives my car. He has never asked me to clean it out, but I know he would appreciate it if I kept it tidier. I have a million excuses for not having completed the task already, but I realize that excuses don't belong in a marriage that wants to go above and beyond. Therefore, I resolve to clean out my car this week and pray for my eyes to be opened to other actions I can take in order to go above and beyond for Jason. I don't want to merely do *what* I can for him, but *all* that I can!

Jesus, You certainly went above and beyond for me. I pray that I can use that as motivation to go above and beyond for my husband. Open my eyes to what would truly bless him, and grant me the motivation to follow through. Be my example and motivation. I pray these things in Your name. Amen.

For the Love of My Husband

Father God, in the powerful name of Jesus Christ, I pray against any acts of the sinful nature (sexual immorality, impurity, and debauchery) that are in my husband's life or temptations he may face. Instead, please help my husband cultivate and produce many fruits of the Spirit in his life. I pray specifically that he would have more love, joy, peace, patience, kindness, goodness, faithfulness, gentleness, and self-control. I pray, Lord, that my husband will daily crucify his sinful nature along with its passions and desires. Help him live by the Spirit, and let him keep in step with the Spirit. Let him not become conceited, provoking or envying anyone (Galatians 5:19, 22–26). Amen.

Week 42

Challenge

I sometimes feel overwhelmed when I read Proverbs 31. I was reading through that chapter recently, and I felt very inadequate compared to the woman described in those verses. Then I sensed the Lord asking me, "Which qualities of hers do you wish to have?" I quickly answered, "All of them!" but He had me focus on just one—if I could add only *one* trait to my life, what would it be? For me, the quality I want to master is found in verse eighteen, which says, "and her lamp does not go out at night." Oftentimes, once my daughter is asleep, I grant myself permission to sit on the couch and watch TV until I'm tired, and then I go to bed. The Proverbs 31 woman, however, goes back to work once her children are asleep, and I desire that same work ethic in my life. My challenge this week is cultivating that *one* quality. I can breathe a sigh of relief, resolving to address one quality at a time rather than trying to frantically apply them all simultaneously. I will move on to another quality once I've mastered Proverbs 31:18b.

How about you? Is there a quality that stands out in the description of the Proverbs 31 woman that you desire in your life? Make that your challenge this week. Don't feel overwhelmed when reading about this amazing woman!

Father God, thank You that You don't require me to master every quality that the Proverbs 31 woman possesses all at once. I appreciate Your patience as I grow one attribute at a time. I pray that You would help me this week as I begin to address the first quality that needs to be applied to my life. I pray that I would master it and that it would become engrained in my daily life. Continue to show me which areas of my life I need to work on so that I can be a better wife every day. In Jesus' name. Amen.

For the Love of My Husband

Abba, thank You for being the ultimate Father. While I know my husband will never be perfect (as You are), I pray that he would model Your love to our children. Grant him wisdom, patience, and guidance as he journeys the path of parenthood. In a world where children are losing their innocence far too early, I pray that he would be their protector and shield. Lord, please show him how to discipline them wisely while loving them unconditionally. Through his words and actions, may they never question his love or Your love. Impress upon his heart the importance of his irreplaceable role as a father, and may he take that role very seriously. May he never raise his voice in anger or his hand in violence or lack of self-control. Please help my husband never to exasperate his children; instead, may he bring them up in the training and instruction of the Lord (Ephesians 6:4). I pray that as our children grow older he can develop a true friendship with them and earn their respect. If my husband is not a father, I pray that he would be a spiritual father to many, finding young men that he can mentor in Your ways (2 Timothy 2:1–2). I ask all of these things in the name of Your Son. Amen.

Week 43

Challenge

My husband and I have spent this past week moving into a new house. Needless to say, it has been hectic. Usually, before writing these weekly devotions, I spend time seeking the Lord's direction for both the challenge and the theme of each prayer. This week, however, I wasn't sure what to write for my challenge, since I have not had much time to ask God what He would like me to improve on as a wife. At first, I was planning to simply write a prayer and forgo the challenge completely, but that's when God led me to this quote by John Piper, "One of the great uses of Twitter and Facebook will be to prove at the Last Day that prayerlessness was not from lack of time."[17]

Wow, I had to read that a few times in order to fully digest it. You see, my excuse for lack of prayer regarding this devotion was that this has been a hectic week, but I was convicted that I somehow found time to update my Facebook page every day. What does that say about my time management? How can I keep up with social networking and yet not have time to pray? My challenge this week is to avoid Facebook and e-mail until I've spent ample time at the feet of Jesus each day, asking Him specifically how I can improve as a wife and praying for my husband. I am going to limit my media intake in general so that I may have more silence to talk (and listen) to my Lord.

Lord, I am sorry for the times when I put other things in front of my time with You. I am specifically sorry for the times when I put things of little value, such as social networking, TV, or other frivolous activities above spending time in prayer. Please forgive me and help me as I seek to implement a new rule of not partaking in those time wasters until I've spent time with You. Help me grasp the importance of the eternal. In Jesus' name, I pray, Amen.

For the Love of My Husband

Father, I pray in the name of Jesus Christ that my husband would be a mighty warrior for You. May he not settle for a mediocre spiritual life, but rather be a sold-out, radical follower of You. Lord, help him stand up to the darkness in his life, in our family, and in the world. I pray that he would become a great enemy of Satan and a threat to the plans of the Evil One. May he be faithful, even to the point of death, so that he will receive the crown of life (Revelations 2:10). I pray that the martyrs around the world, especially those early apostles, would be his heroes in the faith. May he make Hebrews 13:6 his battle cry: "The Lord is my helper; I will not be afraid. What can man do to me?" Amen.

Week 44

Challenge

This week, I began thinking of all the things my husband does for our family. He does big things like moving heavy furniture, fixing appliances, making sure our cars are maintained, paying the bills, and other tasks I never have to worry about because he always takes care of them. Then, I also thought about all the little things he does on a daily basis. For instance, he greets me every morning with a kiss, calls me throughout the day to check in, and he always tells me I look beautiful and that my meals taste great. The little things in a marriage are just as important—if not more so—than the big things, and yet they are often the first to slip away. It doesn't make sense, really, that the actions that require the least amount of time and money are the ones that we quickly neglect.

Personally, I'm usually on top of the big things—making meals, grocery shopping, cleaning, etc.—but I don't always keep up with the little things in my marriage. For each husband, the little things will be different: leaving him love notes, telling him how attractive he is, saying please and thank you (a common courtesy that we would show any stranger), etc. These are often simple and easy tasks, but their importance cannot be ignored. My challenge this week is to focus on the little things that strengthen my marriage and make them a greater priority.

Sweet Jesus, I pray that I would remember small kindnesses in my marriage. Help me remember to be polite to my husband, even for daily things. Please help me show my husband common courtesy and my love daily through the little things I do. Remind me how important words such as "please" and "thank you" actually are. Please continue to work on me, and help me to be a more loving and thoughtful wife. Amen.

For the Love of My Husband

Allow me to introduce this week's prayer with a brief thought. I met with a dear friend this week whose husband served in Iraq for a year. We began talking about the tragic things he saw and experienced while over there. I know there are some nights when Jason comes home from the ER clearly shaken up by what he has seen. Unfortunately, he often witnesses the consequences of man's depravity firsthand by caring for victims of violence, abuse, and neglect. This week's prayer is not limited to soldiers and doctors, but includes anyone who has experienced anything tragic. This prayer can also be applied to anything impure including (although not limited to) pornography. Let's pray for those disturbing images, no matter what they are, to be distant and removed.

Father God, in the name of Jesus Christ I ask you to filter the images and experiences that are within my husband's mind and memory. I pray boldly that any image that haunts him will be removed completely. Instead of those images that steal his peace and joy, I pray that he will dwell on things that are true, noble, right, pure, lovely, admirable, excellent, and praiseworthy (Philippians 4:8). I pray that anything not of You would be completely erased and that You would shield his heart, eyes and mind in any future circumstance. If any future disturbing experience is unavoidable, then I pray that You would comfort him and somehow use it for Your glory by teaching him more about Yourself. I pray that my husband's mind will be a pure place where he would not question You or humanity because of the images he has seen and experienced. Protect my husband in whatever vocation You have called him to and may the images and conversations that play in his head be reflections of You and Your love. We love You, Father, and pray all of these things in Jesus' name. Amen.

Week 45

Challenge

I have to be completely honest and say I have not been the best wife this week. It seems the "me-monster" has totally taken over my actions, attitudes, and words. You see, Jason is currently studying for his examination to become a board-certified physician, a process which has required practically every waking moment of his time. This, of course, leaves me alone to change every diaper, make every meal, entertain my daughter all day long, and go to bed alone while my husband continues studying through the night. Instead of being supportive of him through this challenge, I have focused only on the difficulties of *my* day and the sacrifices *I* have made. I don't know about you, but whenever I'm feeling lonely and unappreciated I tend to have a short temper and take it out on my husband. I know this is wrong, but it is often our human nature to respond in such a way.

The Bible, however, instructs us to respond differently. James 1:19 encourages us to be quick to listen, slow to speak, and slow to become angry. Similarly, Romans 12:18 urges us to live at peace with everyone whenever possible. Certainly those verses are applicable in marriage. My challenge, then, is to apply James 1:19 and Romans 12:18 to my marriage so that I may overcome my selfish tendencies and live at peace with my husband.

Father God, I am sorry for the times when I respond to my husband with harsh words. Help me learn how to better cope with the times in my marriage when I might be feeling lonely or unappreciated. May I never allow myself to use those emotions as an excuse for an angry spirit. Teach me to be quick to listen, slow to speak, and slow to become angry. I pray that I will do my best to live at peace with my husband whenever possible. May I be a supportive and encouraging wife no matter what my day has entailed. Be with me as I attempt to put my husband's needs above my own. In the name of Jesus, I pray. Amen.

For the Love of My Husband

Dear Lord, I pray that my husband would be very careful how he lives. Holy Spirit, help him to grow in wisdom so that he can make the most of every opportunity that comes his way. Train him to hear Your voice and to quiet his mind so that he can see opportunities when they arise. That is especially important because the days are evil (Ephesians 5:15-16). Impress upon him the obligation he has, as a follower of Jesus, to shine the light of truth into every life he touches. Help him to redeem the time so he can live each day to the fullest. In Jesus' name, I pray. Amen.[18]

Week 46

Challenge

There are times in every marriage when life becomes too heavy. Whether you are weighed down by work issues, personal health, child rearing, or extended family circumstances, the stresses of life can be overwhelming. I know that Jason and I have been through seasons where our conversations were entirely serious and we had very little time for laughter. Such an atmosphere can be stifling to a marriage. However, laughter is good for the soul and can greatly reduce stress. In their book *The Love List*, Les and Leslie Parrott recommend that every couple should find something they can laugh about every day.[19] Laughing with your husband creates a special moment of unity which can help any marriage cope during the toughest of circumstances. My challenge this week is to find new ways to usher in a spirit of laughter in our marriage. This can be as simple as watching your favorite comedy, having a Karaoke night at home, or reminiscing about fun memories you have shared. I am excited for this challenge, as I know it will be fun for both of us. Praise God for giving us humor!

Precious Jesus, thank You for the gift of laughter. I pray that You would help me this week to have a sense of humor in all circumstances. Help me be creative in coming up with something that my husband and I can do each day to bring laughter into our home. I pray that I will never laugh at my husband, but only with him. May we be a couple that knows how to laugh together no matter in what season of life we may find ourselves. Amen.

For the Love of My Husband

Father God, I pray that my husband will choose healthy habits for his life. May he fully understand the truth that his body is a temple of the Holy Spirit, and, in response, may he desire to take care of it and use it for Your glory (1 Corinthians 6:19–20). I pray that you would give my husband conviction and self control when it comes to his choice of food and beverage, and while becoming healthy in his eating habits, help him prioritize exercise so that he will be healthy, strong, and full of energy. Lord, I pray that throughout his life, he will never be mastered by any questionable habits (1 Corinthians 6:12), and whether he eats or drinks or whatever he does, may he do it all for Your glory (1 Corinthians 10:31). In Your Son's name, I pray. Amen.

Week 47

Challenge

Once, when Jason and I were on a mission trip to Cuba, he was very nervous because he was planning to preach a sermon in Spanish. As the big moment drew near, I sensed his anxiety was growing, so I prayed with him before he preached and asked God to grant him peace. He later told me that my prayer helped to usher in a spirit of peace for him at that very moment.

I was humbled that the Lord used me as the vessel that allowed Jason to experience the peace he needed at that moment. It is easy to forget how powerful our prayers can be when we don't always see their effects immediately. Let's not take this gift for granted, though. Yes, our prayers can be used to protect our husbands throughout their lives and to build them up over time. However, they can also bring *instant* healing, peace, wisdom, direction, or whatever else our husbands may need at a particular moment, if that is in the Lord's will.

For my challenge this week, I want to pray for my husband's immediate needs and trust that God will provide for him. This will require asking my husband what specific concerns he has each day. Additionally, I must repent of all sin in my life so that my prayers can be most effective. As James 5:16b states, "... pray for each other so that you may be healed. The prayer of a righteous man is powerful and effective." May God use our prayers for our husbands to be powerful tools in their lives, our lives, and our marriages. What an awesome gift the Lord has given us in allowing us to talk to Him!

Father God, I admit there are times when I forget that You can answer prayers the minute they are prayed. You are more powerful than I can truly grasp. I pray that You would help me have a candid conversation with my husband this week where I can discover specific things he needs me to pray for him. Give me the faith to know you can answer those prayers the very minute they are prayed. Be with me, Lord, as I search my own heart and repent of things in my life that do not honor You. I pray that You would motivate me to be the best prayer warrior for my husband that I can possibly be. In Jesus' name. Amen.

For the Love of My Husband

Lord, thank You for the privilege of coming before You in prayer. You are the God of the universe, and yet You delight in taking time to talk with us. I pray for my husband, Lord, and ask that at this very moment, You would grant him whatever he is needing most. I may not even know what it is, but Lord, I pray that You would provide it in a powerful way. May my husband know You as Jehovah Jireh, just as Abraham declared, "The Lord will provide" (Genesis 22:14). Help him to know and experience Your presence and peace. Draw him close to You, as a shepherd gathers his lambs and carries them close to his heart (Isaiah 40:11). I pray these things in Your Son's Name. Amen.

Week 48

Challenge

In the past twenty-four hours, Jason and I have learned that two couples we know are now in the process of divorcing. While we've certainly known marriages that have ended in divorce before, both of these accounts are shocking news to us. One of the couples has been married over ten years and the other over fifteen. They are both Christian couples who have been very active in their churches and, honestly, they are friends we never expected to be in this situation.

This sobering news has reminded Jason and I that we aren't immune to divorce. While we have always said that divorce is not an option in our relationship, we realize it has to be much more than a simple phrase we say. Indeed, it has to be a choice we make every day, and something we are proactive about. My challenge, then, is to be on the offense in affair-proofing and divorce-proofing our marriage. One way this can be accomplished is by establishing guidelines with our husbands that protect the sanctity of our marriage and implementing them in our daily lives. Below are a few of the guidelines that Jason and I abide by in our marriage. You can use this list as a starting point for your marriage:

1. Never walk out of the room in the middle of a discussion/argument.

2. Never ride in a car alone with a member of the opposite sex.

3. Pray together after (and if need be, during) a fight.

4. Have an accountability partner.

5. Never threaten or joke about divorce.

Father God, Satan poses a very real threat to my marriage, and I'm sorry for the times I am not as mindful of that fact as I should be. In the name of Jesus, I ask that You make me even more aware of the attacks on marriage today. I pray that I would make the daily decision to love and be faithful to my husband, no matter what. I also ask that You would help us come up with guidelines which will aid in the protection of our hearts and marriage. Bind Satan from my husband, and our marriage. Amen

For the Love of My Husband

Dear Jesus, I cry out to You, asking that You would protect our marriage from divorce. Never allow it to enter our minds, but if it does, please urge us to reject it immediately, knowing that You hate divorce (Malachi 2:16). I pray that my husband would be committed to our marriage for life. May Your conviction, wisdom, guidance, and grace compel him to remain faithful in our relationship. Encourage my husband not to give up when our marriage faces hardships, which are bound to come. I pray that You would heighten his awareness of Satan's attacks on our marriage, knowing that the Devil only wants to steal, kill, and destroy (John 10:10). Protect us from the Evil One and equip my husband with the tools he needs to overcome Satan's lies and temptations. I love You, Jesus, and I ask that our marriage would reflect Your love and Your faithfulness. Amen.

Week 49

Challenge

Mark Twain said, "I can live for two months on one compliment."[20] I don't know about you, but I can certainly relate to that philosophy. Everyone benefits from both constructive criticism and *genuine* (and that is key) compliments. I have noticed that in my effort to not criticize Jason, I have also not made an intentional effort to compliment him regularly. When I tell him I appreciate something he does for me, that is nice, but I need to make sure I'm expressing my appreciation for the man he *is*, not based on what he *does*. For example, I can focus my compliments on the man God created him to be (personality traits, passions, etc.), the father and husband he is, and the leader/provider he is for our family. This week, my challenge is to focus on who Jason is—not just what he does (right or wrong)—and make sure to compliment what I notice with sincere praise. I'm excited to see how God will show me even more to love about my husband this week, and I will pray it will be a week of blessing for Jason, as well!

Lord, I ask that You would show me more about my husband this week. Allow this to be a week where my love for him increases for who he is and not based on anything he does. As I notice traits about him, I pray that I would be thoughtful enough to compliment him on those. I pray that he would know that I am sincere in my admiration. In Jesus' name I, pray. Amen.

For the Love of My Husband

Father God, no matter what affliction, wandering, bitterness, or gall my husband might remember well, and even when his soul is downcast, may he call to mind and have hope that it is only because of Your great love that he is not consumed, for Your compassions never fail. They are new every morning; great is Your faithfulness! May my husband say to himself, "The Lord is my portion; therefore I will wait for him." Lord, You are good to those who hope in You to those who seek You, and I pray my husband would know that it is good to wait quietly for Your salvation. Give him the strength he needs to bear this yoke (Lamentations 3:19-26). In Your Son's name, I pray. Amen.

Week 50

Challenge

Have you noticed that there are always lessons to be learned and room for growth within marriage? I love that! I know I've said it in the past, but it continues to be true; the more I pray for my husband, the more the Lord is showing me ways to improve as a wife as well! As I look back over this past year, I realize that several of the challenges the Lord has laid on my heart have revolved around my selfishness. While I've been working hard to improve my behaviors in these challenges, I have not been successful at addressing the heart of the matter; that is, the selfishness inside of me. Eric and Leslie Ludy eloquently summarize this struggle by stating, "Marriage is a constant decision to either yield to Christ or yield to your selfish wants."[21] I experience this struggle on a daily basis, and while I might attempt to improve an action or two, I often neglect the reality that when I give into my desires I'm not yielding to Christ, which is a sin. My challenge this week is to memorize the quote above and resolve to yield to Christ.

Lord, I find myself struggling repeatedly with the same sins in my life. Please help me address the root of those sins: my selfishness. May I no longer be content to work on a certain action, but help me work to discover the heart issue behind the action. I pray that my marriage would be a place where I will choose to yield to Christ instead of to my own selfish wants. I know I need Your help to accomplish such a task, and that is my simple, but heartfelt, prayer to You. In Jesus' name. Amen.

For the Love of My Husband

Father God, this world is busy and loud, and I pray amidst all of the distractions that my husband would keep You at the center of his life. I pray that Your presence would be special, significant, and sacred to him. May he never lose sight of Your Holiness, and may he be ever watching and listening for Your direction. I pray he never settles for a status-quo relationship with You, but that He seeks You daily and loves You with all his heart, soul, mind, and strength (Mark 12:30). As he leads our family, please grant him wisdom and discernment so that he may teach us to keep the sacred things sacred. Help him notice the things of You that are all around. May he always recognize Your voice, even when it is only a whisper (1 Samuel 3:8–10, 1 Kings 19:12–13). I pray these things in Jesus' name. Amen.

Week 51

Challenge

One day this week, I was having my quiet time in my bedroom after I had recently cleaned it, and I noticed how focused I was. Normally, I spend my devotion time downstairs in the kitchen, but I was able to spend better quality time with God in the peace and quiet of my own bedroom without the distractions of a barking dog, dishwasher, and scattered toys.

That experience reminded me of a familiar principle I've read in several marriage books: the importance of making the master bedroom a sanctuary. It is wise to keep the bedroom simple, avoiding any technology or even the mail, as those things often invite stress. I've also read that keeping your room clean, adding scented candles, and choosing a relaxing color of paint will add to the feeling of calm. The master bedroom must be a place where the marriage can be rejuvenated after a stressful day. My challenge, then, is to make our bedroom a sanctuary, a special oasis for Jason and I. We are currently living in a rental house, so my creativity may be limited, but I can organize drawers, buy candles, and make every effort to keep our room free from the worries of life.

Precious Lord, help me this week as I make a sanctuary out of our bedroom. I invite Your presence to come fill up our room so that we not only feel rejuvenated, but we can delight in You. I pray that You would help me be creative as I clean, organize, and decorate. I pray that our bedroom would become an oasis for both my husband and myself, and that You would use that room to strengthen us. In Jesus' name. Amen.

For the Love of My Husband

Father God, thank You for Your unconditional love; we don't deserve Your love, favor, or friendship, and yet You offer each so freely to us. While I pray that You will convict my husband when he is in the wrong, I also pray that he will dismiss the lies of Satan that may leave him crippled with guilt. Grant my husband perseverance, striving harder to be a man after Your own heart. Protect his heart from discouragement in his walk with You. When he fails, Lord, I pray that he will dust himself off, get back up, and trust in Your goodness and mercy. May he have a faith like David who once cried out, "How long must I wrestle with my thoughts and every day have sorrow in my heart?" (Psalm 13:2a), but later declared with confidence, "But I trust in Your unfailing love; my heart rejoices in Your salvation. I will sing to the Lord, for He has been good to me" (Psalm 13:5–6). I pray these things in the name of Almighty Jesus. Amen.

Week 52

Challenge

Can you believe it? *We did it!*

We've been joining together in prayer for our husbands for an entire year now! As I reflect over the past twelve months, I am humbled and amazed at what the Lord has accomplished in my marriage and all the work He has yet to do. While I certainly have plenty of room to grow, I am undeniably a much better wife today than I was one year ago. I am noticing all the areas I can improve as a wife rather than focusing on the ways my husband "should" change. I'm also much more faithful in praying for my husband throughout the day with very specific Scriptures and requests. It has been remarkable to see the Lord answer my prayers and to see the love and laughter that has grown in our marriage. I am so glad that you have joined me on this journey of praying for our husbands, and I am confident that your marriage has reaped the rewards of your prayers as well!

Since this is our final week, my challenge is to simply continue. Just because the book ends here does not mean I have to stop creating challenges or prayers. God's expectation for our marriages is much greater than simply avoiding divorce or running on autopilot. Indeed, He has plans for our marriages that are so much more than we could hope or imagine, and He wants to use our marriages for His glory. Let's never give up striving for a better marriage, becoming better wives, and praying more faithfully for our husbands. Thank you again for coming alongside me in this incredible adventure. The journey has only just begun!

Dear Lord, thank You for encouraging me over the past year to grow in my faith and become a better wife. Thank You for Your patience and mercy. Lord, please help me not to give up on my determination to be a better wife. Continue to show me things that I can improve in my own life in order to help strengthen our marriage. I pray that You would continue to keep me faithful in praying a Scripture-based prayer for my husband each week. I pray that I would never grow weary of lifting him up to You. I love you, Jesus, and ask these things in Your name. Amen.

For the Love of My Husband

Father God, thank You for my husband and the gift he is to me and to others. I thank You for bringing us together and for the work You want to do in and through our marriage. Lord, I pray for my husband to be the exceptional husband You have called him to be. I pray that he would desire to know me more intimately. Allow him to listen to me—my needs, my desires, and my heart. While I don't want to grow selfish in our marriage, I do desire to be romanced, which is a desire that comes from You. Help my husband as he tries to meet my needs, but remind me that my greatest fulfillment is from You alone. I pray that I will continually be respectful of him and that, in return, he will be gentle and loving with me (Ephesians 5:33). May he always be open and honest about his emotions, temptations, and hopes. Speak through him as he leads our family, and give him the strength to gently rebuke me when I'm not in accordance with Your will (2 Timothy 4:2). I pray that he would be a protector of me, my reputation, and our marriage. Lord, burden his heart to pray for me daily so that our marriage can be all that You have called it to be. I love You, Jesus, and it is in Your powerful name that I pray. Amen![22]

Endnotes

1. Omartian, Stormie, *The Power of a Praying Wife* (Eugene, 1997), 45.

2. Ludy, Eric and Leslie, *The First 90 Days of Marriage* (Nashville, 2006), 22.

3. Ludy, Eric and Leslie, *The First 90 Days of Marriage* (Nashville, 2006), 8-9.

4. Omartian, Stormie, *The Power of a Praying Wife* (Eugene, 1997), 27.

5. Hahn, Kimberly, *Chosen and Cherished: Biblical Wisdom for Your Marriage* (Cincinnati, 2007), 130-131.

6. Parrott, Les and Leslie, *The Love List* (Grand Rapids, 2002), 65.

7. Ludy, Eric and Leslie, *The First 90 Days of Marriage* (Nashville, 2006), 142-143.

8. Ladd, Karol, *The Power of a Positive Wife* (West Monroe, 2003), 29.

9. Sister Marysia Weber, R.S.M., D.O. "Internet Pornography: An occasion of sin for our time." Sacred Heart Mercy Health Care Center (March 1, 2010).

10. Stone, David, "Keeping a Pure Mind" (Southeast Christian Church, Louisville, 2009).

11. Bethea, Erin, "Fireproof" (Southeast Christian Church, Louisville, 2009).

12. Fraser, Brooke, *Hosanna* (Hillsong United, 2007).

13. Partow, Donna, Becoming the Woman God Wants Me to Be (Grand Rapids, 2008), 29.

14. Kelly, Matthew. "Building Better Families" (Indianapolis, 2009).

15. Mohler, Albert. *"There is a stunning, tragic, sinful, visible lack of testosterone in American evangelicalism, and we are afraid to admit it."* Retrieved from: http://www.facebook.com/#!/AlbertMohler. (October 2009).

16. Barton, Haley Ruth, *Strengthening the Soul of Your Leadership* (Downers Grove, 2008), 201-202.

17. Piper, John, (October 20, 2009), http://twitter.com/JohnPiper/status/5027319857.

18. Partow, Donna, *Becoming the Woman God Wants Me to Be* (Grand Rapids, 2008), 201. Arrangement Mine.

19. Parrott, Les and Leslie, *The Love List* (Grand Rapids, 2002), 33.

20. Parrott, Les and Leslie, *The Love List* (Grand Rapids, 2002), 59.

21. Ludy, Eric and Leslie, *The First 90 Days of Marriage* (Nashville, 2006), 27.

22. Wolfe, Dana Lynn, *Top 10 Things to Pray For Your Husband* (Pottstown, 2007).

CPSIA information can be obtained at www.ICGtesting.com
Printed in the USA
LVOW111511230212

270119LV00007B/137/P